Baedeker
Tenerife
La Palma/Gomera/Hierro

Baedeker's

TENERIFE

Imprint

Cover picture: View of Mount Teide

94 colour photographs
3 special plans, 5 town plans, 2 drawings, 1 map of communications, 1 map of islands

Text: Birgit Borowski

Editorial work:
Baedeker Stuttgart

English Language Edition:
Alec Court

Design and layout:
Creativ GmbH, Ulrich Kolb, Stuttgart

General direction:
Dr Peter Baumgarten, Baedeker Stuttgart

Cartography:
Franz Kaiser, Sindelfingen; Gert Oberländer, Munich;
Mairs Geographischer Verlag GmbH & Co., Ostfildern-Kemnat (map of islands)

English translation:
James Hogarth

Source of illustrations:
Bader (21), Bohnacker (1), Borowski (61), Brödel (2), Gugel und Macher (1), Historia-Photo (2), Linde (3), Museo Arqueológico de Tenerife (2), ZEFA (1).

To make it easier to locate the various sights listed in the "A to Z" section of the Guide, their coordinates on the large map of the islands are shown in red at the head of each entry.

Following the tradition established by Karl Baedeker in 1844, sights of particular interest are distinguished by either one or two asterisks.

Only a selection of hotels, restaurants and shops can be given: no reflection is implied, therefore, on establishments not included.

The symbol ⓘ on a town plan indicates the local tourist office from which further information can be obtained. The post-horn symbol indicates a post office.

In a time of rapid change it is difficult to ensure that all the information given is entirely accurate and up to date, and the possibility of error can never be completely eliminated. Although the publishers can accept no responsibility for inaccuracies and omissions, they are always grateful for corrections and suggestions for improvement.

Contents

Preface

This pocket guide to Tenerife, La Palma, Gomera and Hierro is one of the new generation of Baedeker guides.

Baedeker pocket guides, illustrated throughout in colour, are designed to meet the needs of the modern traveller. They are quick and easy to consult, with the principal places of interest described in alphabetical order, and the information is presented in a format that is both attractive and easy to follow.

The present guide is devoted to the western Canary Islands: in the first place Tenerife, the largest and most important island in the group, together with the smaller islands – less developed for tourism but scenically no less interesting – of La Palma, Gomera and Hierro. The guide is in three parts. The first part gives a general account of the islands, their geography, climate, flora and fauna, population, art, economy and transport, notable personalities, history and the culture of the early inhabitants. In the second part the places and features of tourist interest are described, and the third part contains a variety of practical information. Both the sights and the practical information are listed in alphabetical order.

The Baedeker pocket guides are noted for their concentration on essentials and their convenience of use. They contain numerous specially drawn plans and colour illustrations; and at the end of the book is a large map making it easy to locate the various places described in the "A to Z" section of the guide with the help of the coordinates given at the head of each entry.

Facts and Figures

General

This guide is concerned with the western Canary islands of Tenerife, La Palma, Gomera and Hierro. The eastern Canary islands of Gran Canaria, Fuerteventura and Lanzarote are described in the Baedeker/AA pocket guide "Gran Canaria".

Canary Islands

The Canary Islands (in Spanish Islas Canarias) are a group of seven major islands and six smaller ones in the Atlantic, lying between 96 and 304 km (60 and 190 miles) off the north-western coast of Africa (Morocco; Western Sahara) and some 1120 km (700 miles) from the Spanish mainland (Cádiz), between latitude 27°38' and 29°35' N and between longitude 13°20' and 18°9' W. The whole archipelago extends for 496 km (310 miles) from east to west and 200 km (125 miles) from north to south.

The western islands of Tenerife (area 2057 sq. km (794 sq. miles)), La Palma (728 sq. km (281 sq. miles)), Gomera (378 sq. km (146 sq. miles)) and Hierro (277 sq. km (107 sq. miles)) form the province of Santa Cruz de Tenerife (chief town Santa Cruz), the eastern islands of Gran Canaria (1532 sq. km (592 sq. miles)), Fuerteventura (1731 sq. km (668 sq. miles)) and Lanzarote (795 sq. km (307 sq. miles)) the province of Las Palmas de Gran Canaria (chief town Las Palmas).

The two provinces make up the Autonomous Region of the Canary Islands (Comunidad Autónoma de Canarias), with Las Palmas and Santa Cruz alternating as capital of the region.

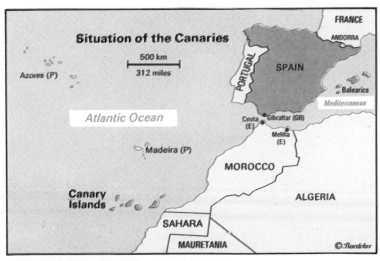

General

Common features with other island groups

Together with the Azores, Madeira and the Cape Verde Islands the Canaries belong to the Macaronesian Islands ("Blessed Islands"), which all show common features in flora and fauna, are all of volcanic origin and have similar topographic patterns.

Origins of the name

It is not known for certain how the Canary Islands got their name. The designation "Isla Canaria" appears for the first time on a Spanish chart of 1339. In antiquity the group was known as the Blessed or Fortunate Islands; later the name Canaria was applied by Pliny the Elder (A.D. 23–79) to the island now known as Gran Canaria. Pliny related the name (*canis*=dog) to the large dogs which lived on the island. There were certainly dogs in the Canaries in Pliny's time, though they were not unusually large. The Romans associated the islands with the kingdom of the dead which lay in the west; and it is possible that this had something to do with the name, for in ancient mythological conceptions the dead were conducted into the underworld by dogs. It has also been suggested that the bird known to the Romans as *canora* (singing bird) may have lived on the islands. Still another possibility is that the name may have come from the Cape of Canauria (probably Cape Bojador) on the African coast.

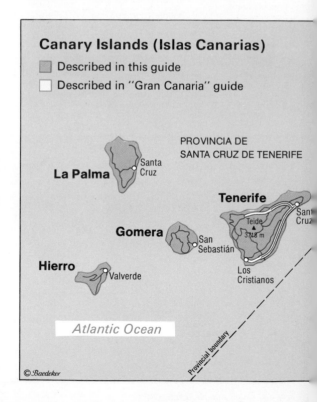

Canary Islands (Islas Canarias)

■ Described in this guide
□ Described in "Gran Canaria" guide

PROVINCIA DE
SANTA CRUZ DE TENERIFE

La Palma
Santa
Cruz

Tenerife
San
Cruz
Teide
▲
3718 m

Gomera
San
Sebastián

Hierro
Valverde

Los
Cristianos

Atlantic Ocean

Provincial boundary

© Baedeker

The two provinces of the Canaries have governors appointed by the Central Government, with their headquarters in Santa Cruz and Las Palmas respectively. The Cabildo Insular (Island Council) has, however, certain powers of self-government, with responsibility among other things for health services, roads, water-supply and culture. The local government authority is the ayuntamiento (municipality).

The Canaries were granted these powers of self-government in 1982 under the Spanish policy of decentralization.

Many people in the Canaries feel that these powers of self-government are insufficient, and in recent years the degree of independence to be aimed at has been a principal theme of local political controversy. The Union of the Canarian People (Unión del Pueblo Canario, UPC) campaigns for complete independence, but is a long way from commanding a majority; and radical separatist organizations such as the Movement for Self-Determination and Independence (MPAIAC) find little popular support. A large proportion of the population would favour an extensive measure of self-government within a Spanish federal state. This appeals particularly to the poorer classes of the population, who suffer most from the economic

Administration

Independence movements

crisis, and in their eyes the mainland Spaniards are responsible for all their troubles. Many of their grievances date from the period of Franco's dictatorship, when the Canaries were scandalously neglected.

Origins of the archipelago

In geological terms the Canary Islands are quite young. The age of the eastern islands of Lanzarote and Fuerteventura is estimated to be between 16 and 20 million years and that of Gran Canaria between 13 and 14 million years, while the western islands are thought to have come into being even later – Tenerife and Gomera perhaps between 8 and 12 million years ago, La Palma and Hierro between 2 and 3 million years ago. The variations in the topography of the individual islands confirm this picture of a reduction in age from east to west. Erosional forces have evidently been longer at work on Lanzarote and Fuerteventura with their low rounded hills than on the western Canaries with their rugged and mountainous terrain.

It is well established that all the islands are of volcanic origin, and the theory of "hot spots" has been put forward to explain how they came into being. At certain points in the earth's mantle – always the same points – magma collects in the course of millions of years and is then discharged in volcanic eruptions. A process of this kind gave rise in the first place to the islands of Lanzarote and Fuerteventura. As a result of continental drift (which is thought to take place in this region at the rate of between 2 and 3 cm ($\frac{3}{4}$ and $1\frac{3}{8}$ in) a year) they moved gradually farther east. Magma then accumulated at the same spot and thrust its way upward to form other volcanic islands, ending with Hierro.

This theory is still the subject of controversy. What is certain, however, is that the earlier view that the Canaries, or at least Lanzarote and Fuerteventura, were once part of the African continent has been disproved.

Formation of the Canaries

The "hot spot" theory

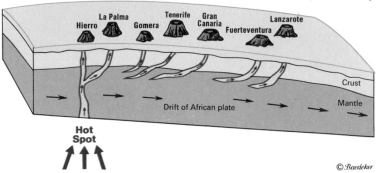

Hierro · La Palma · Gomera · Tenerife · Gran Canaria · Fuerteventura · Lanzarote

Crust

Mantle

Drift of African plate

Hot Spot

© Baedeker

Volcanic activity

There have been repeated volcanic eruptions in the Canaries, continuing into our own day; the most recent have been the eruptions on La Palma in 1949 and 1971. On Tenerife there were eruptions of Chinyero (10 km (6 miles) north-west of the Pico de Teide) in 1909 and Chahorra (south-west of the Pico Viejo) in 1798. It is not surprising, therefore, that volcanism has left its mark on the topography of the islands. Tenerife and La Palma are dominated by their central volcanoes, and all over the islands can be seen extensive flows of black lava. The greatest variety of volcanic phenomena is to be found in the Caldera de las Cañadas on Tenerife, a kind of gigantic open-air museum of different volcanic rocks. The best known of the eruptive rocks is the bluish-black basalt. Trachyte is light coloured, with a rough surface; phonolite is greyish green. Obsidian, a dark-coloured grassy rock, is named after its discoverer, a Roman named Obsidius. Pumice, which has the astonishing property of floating in water, is a froth-like rock produced by the formation of gas bubbles in slow-flowing lava.

The expanses of infertile lava, often still looking quite fresh, are known as *malpaís* (bad lands). After a period of weathering, however, the lava forms a soil which can be successfully cultivated if climatic conditions are favourable. Volcanic ash in particular contains nutrients essential for plant life. The people of the Canaries have learned by experience how to make the best use of the properties of the volcanic rock; thus pumice and lapilli (fragments of volcanic rock ranging in size between a pea and a nut) are used to retain moisture in the soil (see Economy and Transport).

Tenerife, the largest of the Canaries, is shaped like an isosceles triangle pointing north-east, with the Pico de Teide (3718 m (12,199 ft)) in its centre. Encircling the peak is the Caldera de las Cañadas, a gigantic collapsed crater. To the north-east extends the Cumbre Dorsal, which slopes gradually down from 2200 m (7200 ft) to 1700 m (5600 ft) and then falls sharply to the plateau of La Laguna (550–600 m (1800–2000 ft)). The north-eastern tip of the island is occupied by the rugged Anaga Hills, which, like the Teno Hills in the extreme west of the island, consist of older basaltic rocks. The two ranges of hills are believed at one time to have been separate islands which were linked with one another by a later volcanic eruption. They divide Tenerife into two totally different topographic zones; while the hill slopes in the north are covered with a luxuriant growth of vegetation the country to the south is desertic in character.

Topography of Tenerife

The hills are broken up by *barrancos* (gorges), which with one exception (the Barranco del Infierno) are no longer traversed by watercourses. In spite of this the lower reaches frequently offer favourable conditions for agriculture. On the flanks of the hills extend a number of broad and fertile valleys such as the Valle de la Orotava in the north and the Valle de Güimar in the south.

The rugged cliff-fringed coasts of the island are relieved here and there by small coves with beaches of black or light-coloured sand. The only stretch of low-lying coastal land is in the south.

For descriptions of the topography of Gomera, Hierro and La Palma see the entries on those islands in the "A to Z" section.

Topography of Gomera, Hierro and La Palma

Climate

The Canaries have a warm temperate climate – milder and more agreeable than would normally be expected in these latitudes. It is mainly influenced by the trade winds, but also by the zone of high pressure over the Azores and the cool Canary Current. The varying forms of relief in the western Canaries give rise to minor climatic peculiarities (see "A to Z", Gomera, Hierro, La Palma). There are, however, considerably greater differences between the northern and southern halves of the individual islands.

Temperature

Temperature variations over the year are remarkably slight. Thus the average temperature in the coastal regions of Tenerife in January, the coldest month, is 17·8 °C (64·0 °F) – absolute minimum 10·5 °C (50·9 °F), absolute maximum 26·5 °C (79·7 °F), and in August, the hottest month, 24·2 °C (75·6 °F) – absolute minimum 17·2 °C (63·0 °F), absolute maximum 40·4 °C (104·7 °F). In the hill regions there is, of course, a temperature gradation according to altitude. In July and August the weather pattern is sometimes affected by three- or four-day heat waves coming from the Sahara.
Water temperatures are about 19 °C (66 °F) in winter and may reach 22 °C (72 °F) in summer.

Rainfall

Rainfall is mainly confined to the winter months, when it is brought by cyclones from northern latitudes. In the southern parts of the islands, however, there is little rain even in winter. On the north coasts the average annual rainfall is about 500 mm (20 in); in the central regions it rises to 600–800 mm (24–31 in) and in the mountains falls again to 300 mm (12 in). The snowline is about 1200 m (3900 ft).

Trade winds

Westerly current

Tropic of Cancer

NE Trade winds

Easterly current

Equator (ITC)

Easterly current

SE trade winds

Tropic of Capricorn

Westerly current

© Baedeker (after Flohn)

Over the western Canaries a bank of cloud regularly forms at medium altitudes in the early morning, dispersing towards evening. The clouds rarely bring rain, but they do bring moisture in the form of mist and dew. The clouds are caused throughout almost the whole of the year by the trade winds blowing from the north-east, usually at force 4.
In contrast to other climate influences the trade winds are constant. Their circulation begins at the Equator, where the sun's warming influence on the earth is at its highest (intra-tropical convergence, ITC). The warm air masses rise, becoming gradually cooler, and flow at a height of 12–15 km (7½–9½ miles) towards the Pole. After cooling still further they sink down to the surface of the earth about latitude 30° and flow close to the ground towards the Equator. As a result of the rotation of the earth, however, the current of air is diverted from its original direction, flowing from the north-east in the Northern Hemisphere and from the south-east in the Southern Hemisphere. Above about 1500 m (4900 ft) the winds are warm and dry, below that altitude moist and rather cooler. So long as the separation between the upper and the lower layers (the "inversion" of the winds) is preserved there is little formation of cloud; but when the winds come up against a sufficiently high hill the inversion is disturbed. The cool moist lower current is halted on the slopes exposed to the sun, becomes warmer and rises, whereupon it is cooled again and

condenses, and clouds then form between 600 m (2000 ft) and 1700 m (5500 ft). (It follows that there is no formation of clouds during the night.)

With the trade winds blowing from the north-east, the southern parts of the islands are not affected in this way but are exposed only to warm dry winds blowing down from the hills.

The influence of the trade winds is less marked in winter. The sun's rays strike the Northern Hemisphere at a much more acute angle (whereas in the Southern Hemisphere the sun is vertically over the Tropic of Capricorn on 22 December). The zone subject to the trade winds then moves farther south, and the Canaries come under the influence of Atlantic troughs of low pressure.

Water-supply has been a perennial problem on the Canaries. The scanty rainfall seeps away in the porous volcanic soil and collects in underground cavities with floors of impervious rock. These reservoirs are now tapped by boring and the water is distributed to users in some 1000 irrigation channels with a total length of some 1500 km (930 miles).

Water-supply

Flora and Fauna

Flora

The flora of the Canaries is unique in two respects. On the one hand there are found here within a relatively small area species of plants from almost every vegetation zone in the world; on the other hand there is a strikingly high proportion of endemic species (plants which are found only here). Altogether the flora of the Canaries comprises almost 2000 species, fully 30 per cent of which are endemic. In the Mediterranean region, the Alps and southern Russia numerous fossils of fruits and leaves have been found which show that plants now occurring only in the Canaries were once common there, too. The climatic catastrophes of the Late Tertiary era (the beginning of the Ice Age, the drying up of the Sahara) drove the subtropical flora of the period from its previous habitat, but the isolated situation of the Canaries allowed it to survive there. Moreover the considerable differences in altitude on the islands made it possible for plants to adapt to changing climatic conditions by migrating to different altitudes.

General

Major factors in the establishment of different vegetation zones have been differences in altitude and the influence of the trade winds. The lowest level is arid and desertic, with a vegetation which includes the Canary date-palm and succulents such as the pillar euphorbia. This zone reaches up to as much as 1000 m (3300 ft) in the south of the islands but in the north it is confined to the coastal region. Here the natural vegetation includes junipers and the dragon tree between 200 m (650 ft) and 600 m (2000 ft), followed by laurels above 600 m (2000 ft). The zone of evergreen deciduous forest gives place at 1100 m (3600 ft) to the fayal-brezal formation (*faya* = bog myrtle, *brezo* = tree heath). The tree heath can grow to a height of 15 m (50 ft), but it may sometimes be no more than a shrub or dwarf shrub. The fayal-brezal formation together with the zone of laurel woodland is also known as the Monte Verde

Vegetation zones

zone. In the northern half of the western Canaries the zone of pine forests begins at 1500 m (4900 ft), but in the south the Canary pine grows from 1000 m (3300 ft) upwards. In both north and south this zone ends at 2000 m (6500 ft). Between 2000 m and 2700 m (8900 ft) the characteristic species are *retama* (Teide broom) and *codeso*, a low-growing shrub with yellow flowers. Beyond this is the *violeta* (violet) formation, with few species. Here with luck you may find the Teide violet discovered by Alexander von Humboldt (flowering in May–June).

Dragon tree

The most striking and most characteristic plant in the Canaries, with its tall stem and many-branched crown, is the dragon tree (*Dracaena draco*). It belongs to the Liliaceae and is closely related to the yucca. Some specimens grow to a height of 20 m (65 ft). The dragon tree's branches end in a cluster of long dark green sword-shaped leaves. Since the tree sends out branches only after its first blossoming, there is little resemblance between the young tree and an older one like the mighty dragon tree of Icod. Dragon trees do not form annual rings, and the age of a tree can be determined only by the number of branches – an unreliable method, since the branches are put out at irregular intervals. For the indigenous inhabitants of the Canaries the dragon tree had special significance; they used the resin from its stem, which turned red on exposure to the air (dragon's blood), as an ingredient in their healing salves.

Canary date-palm

The Canary date-palm (*Phoenix canariensis*) has spread from the Canaries all over the Mediterranean. It is closely related to the date-palm of North Africa and the Arab countries, but is

Dragon tree

Date-palm

shorter and sturdier and has a fuller and more decorative crown with larger and more luxuriant leaves. The small dates it produces are woody and inedible. On Tenerife it is mainly found in parks and bordering streets; large groves of palms are to be seen mainly on Gomera.

The Canary pine (*Pinus canariensis*) is a prominant feature of the landscape on Tenerife, Hierro and La Palma. Its long and flexible needles always occur in threes. Its hard, reddish-coloured, heartwood (Spanish *tea*) has long been (and still is) used in the construction of wooden ceilings and balconies. At the pine's altitude of between 1000 m (3300 ft) and 2000 m (6600 ft) the moisture in the clouds brought by the trade winds condenses on its branches and drips down its needles into the ground. The water thus obtained is not merely sufficient for the tree's own needs but makes a substantial contribution to the island's water-supply.

Canary pine

A typical representative of the succulents is the prickly pear (*Opuntia ficus indica*), which was brought to the Canaries in the 16th c. It is commonly found on hillsides up to medium altitude. Its fruits are edible and are offered for sale. On this plant is reared the cochineal insect, which yields a red colouring substance, but cochineal is now produced commercially only on the eastern Canary island of Lanzarote.

Prickly pear

In addition to the prickly pear and some species of agave the Spanish conquerors also introduced to the Canaries a number of luxuriantly flowering ornamental plants, and oleanders, hibiscus and bougainvilleas are now to be seen in parks and

Ornamental plants

Poinsettia   *Strelitzia*

gardens all over the islands. The red poinsettias, which form dense bushes 3–4 m (10–13 ft) high, are a ubiquitous feature of the landscape in northern Tenerife during the winter months. Particularly exotic is the strelitzia or bird-of-paradise flower with its unusual inflorescences.

Useful plants

The natural vegetation pattern of the islands was also altered by introduction of various food plants, and the land at lower levels is now extensively planted with bananas, fruit trees, vegetables and vines.

The banana

The most important food crop on the islands is the banana. Since the end of the 19th c. a small species imported from Indochina (*Musa cavendishii*) which is not sensitive to weather conditions has been cultivated on Tenerife. The stem of the banana plant, made up of long, stiff, sappy sheaths, terminates in long fibrous leaves. When the plant is about a year old it produces a large club-shaped inflorescence, with the female flowers in the lower part and the male flowers in the upper part. Depending on the amount of sunshine and the altitude (bananas flourish in the Canaries up to 300–400 m (1000–1300 ft)), the fruit ripens in 4–6 months. A bunch of bananas weighs on average 25–30 kg (55–65 lb), and occasionally as much as 60 kg (130 lb). After producing the fruit the plant dies, but not before producing fresh shoots. The strongest of the shoots is preserved, and after another year puts forth a bud as long as a man's arm.

Environmental influences

The tourist boom and the extensive building developments associated with it have had serious consequences for the native flora of the islands, and many endemic species are threatened with extinction.
Large-scale felling of the forests has also had devastating effects on ecological conditions. In the past great expanses of forest have been cleared to provide land for cultivation, and it is only within the last few decades that efforts have been made to replant the forests, which are not only essential to the islands' water-supply but also help to prevent erosion of the hillsides. It is to be hoped that the national parks on Tenerife, Gomera and La Palma will also contribute to the preservation of the unique flora of the islands.

Fauna

The fauna of the Canaries shows a much narrower range of species than their flora – though here, too, endemic species are relatively numerous.
There are no large mammals – only rabbits, hedgehogs and bats. It is reassuring for visitors that there are no scorpions or poisonous snakes. Lizards, however, are everywhere to be seen, and an occasional slow-worm, a lizard with atrophied legs. A relic of the Tertiary era is the giant lizard, *Gallotia simonyi*, now found only on Hierro; some specimens of this endangered species reach a length of up to 1 m (40 in).
Birds are well represented – blackbirds, bluetits, a species of robin, chaffinches, woodpeckers, various species of pigeons, buzzards, kestrels, seagulls, ibises. Occasionally the fluting song of the *capirote*, the Canary nightingale, can be heard. But visitors who expect to see the familiar yellow canary living in

the wild on the islands from which it takes its name will be disappointed; there is only one inconspicuous wild form, the Canary finch, with greyish-green plumage and no great talent as a songster.

There are innumerable endemic species of insects. Butterfly-lovers are well catered for; particularly striking are the Canary admiral and the brimstone, with orange-red fore-wings. On La Palma silkworms are now being reared on an increased scale.

The waters round the Canaries contain an abundance of fish. Salmon, cuttlefish, moray, bass, ray and sprat are merely a few of the numerous species represented. No dangerous sharks have been seen near the coast, but sometimes swarms of dolphins accompany the ferries.

Population

The Autonomous Region of the Canary Islands has a total population of just under 1,500,000 of whom some 600,000 live on Tenerife, 72,000 on La Palma, 20,000 on Gomera and 6000 on Hierro. The density of population on Tenerife is 287 to the square kilometre (743 to the square mile), or more than three times as much as in mainland Spain. The area with the largest concentration of population in the western Canaries is Santa Cruz de Tenerife (pop. 190,000).

General

The people of the Canaries are predominantly Roman Catholic, with only small minorities of Protestants.

It has been shown by anthropologists that the Canarians differ in some respects from other Spaniards, with many features that point to their descent from the indigenous inhabitants of the islands (see Early Population).

After the end of Franco's dictatorship the social problems of the Canaries were very evident. It was estimated that at that time the illiteracy rate in some villages was as high as 50 per cent. It now averages between 8 and 12 per cent – still higher than in many other parts of Spain.

Social problems

Unemployment is also higher than in mainland Spain. The number of registered unemployed in the Canaries is at present 120,000, but the real figure is likely to be considerably higher. It is estimated that on Tenerife something like a quarter of the population, varying according to the season, are out of work. Depending on the length of time they have been in employment they can expect to receive an unemployment allowance amounting to 48 per cent of their last pay for a period of 12 to 18 months.

In the past the usual way to escape from poverty was to emigrate, particularly to South America: there are said, for example, to be some 300,000 Canarians living in Caracas (Venezuela) alone. The South American States are now taking very few immigrants, and this has still further aggravated the unemployment problem in the Canaries. There is still, however, a shortage of skilled workers, since many of them have left for the Spanish mainland, attracted by the better prospects there.

As in the rest of Spain, Castilian (Castellano) is the language of government and business, and most Canarians also speak pure Castilian, though they tend, like the South Americans, to soften or elide the letter s.

Language

19

On Tenerife English is spoken in the tourist areas. On La Palma, Gomera and Hierro a smattering of Spanish will be found useful.

Art and Culture

Art

Little is left of the art of the ancient Canarians. Apart from a few pieces of pottery and animal figures (see Early Population) visitors will find no artistic evidence of the indigenous culture of the archipelago.

In the centuries following the Spanish conquest numbers of churches and modest public buildings were erected, closely following European and particularly Spanish architectural and artistic traditions. Although there are no outstanding masterpieces there are some buildings of notable quality, in very varying styles.

Gothic influences are only occasionally found in the Canaries (e.g. in the sacristy of the Iglesia de San Salvador in Santa Cruz de la Palma), but there are many examples of Renaissance architecture. Following ancient architectural forms, they make a clear distinction between the different storeys of a building (Town Hall, Santa Cruz de la Palma).

The Mudéjar style, which shows a mingling of Moorish with Gothic or Renaissance forms, was developed in Spain by the Mudéjars (the "Moors who were allowed to stay"), but also by Christian architects influenced by the Moorish style. Its main characteristics are horseshoe arches, stalactitic vaulting and stucco ornament.

The Mudéjar style developed into Plateresque, which came into vogue in Spain at the end of the 15th c. In this style the façades of buildings were covered with a profusion of intricate ornament. A particular variant of the style developed in the Canaries, and many buildings were given ceilings of Canary pine, richly carved and sometimes painted.

In the 17th c. Baroque came to the Canaries. An example of this style is the Iglesia de Santa Catalina in Tacoronte. In addition many churches were equipped with Baroque furnishings and works of art.

The Neo-classical style which came in during the second half of the 18th c. left its mark mainly on the façades of buildings, which were strictly articulated and, in comparison with Baroque architecture, given little in the way of sculptural decoration (Town Hall, La Orotava).

The characteristic feature of 19th c. architecture is the mingling of a variety of styles modelled on the buildings of the past.

Since the middle of this century there has been a regular building boom in the Canaries, particularly on Tenerife. Innumerable large hotels have been built all over the island; brand-new tourist resorts such as Playa de las Américas have been created and the process is still continuing. These developments, often of dubious architectural quality, have given rise to some controversy on the islands, and some attempts have been made to give new developments a more human face.

Particularly notable in this respect has been the work of the Canarian architect César Manrique (see Notable Personalities).

A typical wooden balcony

In all periods the Canaries were notable for fine woodcarving.

In most of the major churches in the archipelago there are statues in wood by the greatest Canarian sculptor, Luján Pérez (1756–1815). Mention has already been made of the richly decorated wooden ceilings to be found in both sacred and secular buildings. Perhaps the most typical features of Canarian architecture, however, are the beautiful wooden balconies. A stroll round La Laguna or La Orotava will reveal numbers of these narrow balconies, all with different forms of decoration.

An essential part of the life of the Canarians is played by their fiestas. As a rule these are of religious origin and are held in honour of one of the island saints. They usually begin with a religious procession, which is followed by more secular diversions.

Music features largely in these ceremonies. The songs, passionate in rhythm and melody, are usually accompanied by the *timple*, a small stringed instrument.

Folk traditions

In almost every place of any size there is a ring for Canarian wrestling contests (*lucha canaria*). In this ring, 9–10 m (30–33 ft) in diameter, the contest is between two wrestlers, each belonging to a twelve-man team. The winner is the first to achieve a fall.

The *juego del palo*, a contest like singlesticks but played with two sticks, calls for extraordinary dexterity. Each contestant has to attack his opponent and ward off his blows, moving the body as little as possible.

Traditional sports

Economy and Transport

In the northern parts of the western Canaries the predominant crop is bananas. This is a fairly recent development, for in past centuries there was a succession of different monocultures. After the Spanish conquest sugar-cane was the principal crop, but competition from the cheaper sugar of Central America led to the decline of Canarian sugar-cane cultivation. The main product then became wine, and in the 17th and 18th c. the heavy Malvasía (Malmsey) of the Canaries was much prized at European Courts. But tastes changed, and in the 19th c. there was a switch to the rearing of the cochineal insect, a parasite of cactuses yielding a red colouring substance which flourished on the newly planted fields of prickly pear. With the development of aniline dyes, however, the economic importance of the cochineal insect declined, and cochineal is now used only in the manufacture of lipsticks and for colouring aperitifs, aerated drinks and sweets. The cochineal insect is still reared on a modest scale on Tenerife and above all on the eastern Canary island of Lanzarote. The ailing economy of the islands was then given a boost by the cultivation of the banana – a small species (*Musa cavendishii*), less vulnerable to weather conditions, which was brought in from Indochina and by about 1890 was being grown on a considerable scale in Tenerife. In recent years banana-growing, too, has been in a state of crisis. Since the small Canary banana, tasty though it is, looks puny in comparison with its competitors in Central and South America, it is now almost unsaleable on the European market, and the costs of production are much higher than in other countries. The Spanish Government has, therefore, been

Agriculture

In the north of the islands: bananas, bananas everywhere

compelled to subsidise Canary bananas by guaranteeing a market, and 96 per cent of the total crop (some 400,000 tonnes) goes to the Spanish mainland. This, however, is only a temporary solution. Since Spain became a member of the EEC a transitional period for the Canary banana has been agreed, after which bananas from other countries are to be admitted to the Spanish market.

The people of the Canaries are now beginning to adjust to the new economic situation. Banana plantations are now increasingly giving place to exotic vegetables and cut flowers; pineapple plantations, for example, are operating successfully. Banana-growing is now mainly concentrated in the northern parts of the islands. The main crops in the south are tomatoes and potatoes, together with maize, wheat, barley, fruit, vegetables and fodder plants for domestic consumption. Wine production is of lesser importance.

Since rainfall in the Canaries is relatively low, and in the south almost non-existent, extensive irrigation systems and special dry-farming methods are essential. While the huge banana plantations in the north are dependent on expensive irrigation schemes, agriculture in the south of Tenerife is based on Canarian techniques of dry farming. The soil is mixed or covered with volcanic rock (lapilli, pumice), which, being porous, is able to store water. It also increases condensation immediately above the ground, since it takes in heat during the day and cools rapidly at night. Thanks to these special properties the rock keeps the soil perpetually moist to a depth of 25–30 cm (10–12 in).

Malvasía wine grapes

A "hand" of bananas

Stock-farming is of secondary importance, and locally reared cattle and pigs meet only part of the islands' requirements. Herds of goats are a ubiquitous feature of the landscape. Dromedaries are still used to some extent as working animals, particularly in the south of Tenerife.

Fishing (particularly tunny-fishing) is practised round all the islands.

In general agriculture, once the main means of subsistence, is now declining in importance on Tenerife and to a lesser extent on the other western Canary islands. It now accounts for barely 10 per cent of the gross domestic product, and the local production of foodstuffs covers only 25 per cent of domestic consumption.

Dromedary

Industry contributes about 25 per cent of the gross domestic product. A major part is played by the large oil-refinery at Santa Cruz de Tenerife, the second largest in Spain, which processes Venezuelan oil, partly for local consumption and partly for supplying ocean-going vessels. There are also a number of medium-sized woodworking, papermaking and fish-processing factories. Craft goods (embroidery, etc.) are produced in small establishments – some very small indeed.

Industry

Since 1852 the Canaries have been a free trade (duty-free) zone, and this has given a great boost to trade. Shortage of water, raw materials and electric power, however, put a brake on economic development, and as a result the balance of trade has long been in deficit. Imports, principally from mainland Spain, are increasing, and there are also considerable imports from West Germany (beer, milk, butter, fruit juices, etc.).

Commerce

Economy and Transport

Transport

In contrast to La Palma, Gomera and Hierro, Tenerife has an excellent road system, with four-lane motorways running from Santa Cruz de Tenerife to the north and south of the island. There are no railways, and public transport is confined to buses. There are regular ferry services between the islands, and the port of Santa Cruz plays a major part in the economy of the archipelago, as well as being a key point in Spain's overseas trade.

The western Canaries have two international airports, both on Tenerife. Almost all charter flights use the Reina Sofia Airport in the south of the island, which came into operation in 1978. The airports on La Palma and Hierro handle only domestic flights. It is planned shortly to begin work on the construction of an airport on Gomera.

Tourism

While agriculture and industry are declining or stagnating there has been a great boom in tourism in recent years, and it now accounts for 67 per cent of the gross domestic product. An annual 1·6 million visitors, mainly from Britain and Germany but also from mainland Spain, come to Tenerife alone. Many of them have built second homes on the islands, sending land prices rocketing.

The tourist infrastructure is being developed all the time. But the number of potential visitors is not unlimited, and some hotels are almost empty during the summer months.

Ambitious plans are also under consideration for the smaller islands in the western Canaries, which have hitherto catered only for small numbers of individual visitors. On Hierro, for example, a tenfold increase in the number of beds available, at present barely 300, is planned over the next few years.

Notable Personalities

Jean de Béthencourt, a Norman, was entrusted by Henry III of Castile with the task of conquering the Canaries. His lieutenant was Gadifer de la Salle, with whom he had taken part in a "Crusade" against Tunis in 1390.

Jean de Béthencourt
(1359–1425)

The two men assembled an expeditionary fleet, which sailed from La Rochelle in 1402. When Béthencourt at last saw the first islands in the archipelago he named them in delight, bare and rocky though they were, Alegranza (Joy) and Graciosa (the Beautiful). Soon afterwards the adventurers landed on Lanzarote and were able to capture it in a relatively short time. Then Béthencourt returned to Spain for reinforcements, and Henry bestowed on him the title of "King of the Canary Islands": whereupon Gadifer, offended, took no further part in the enterprise. In consequence Béthencourt was solely responsible for the conquest of Fuerteventura, which was achieved in 1405, and gave the name of Betancuria to the town which he founded as its capital. Soon afterwards he also took Hierro. Thereafter he settled the two islands with peasants from Normandy and Spain, and the native population was rigorously converted to Christianity.

In 1406 Béthencourt appointed his nephew Maciot de Béthencourt Viceroy of the islands and returned to France, where he died in 1425 in his castle in Granville.

Beatriz de Bobadilla, a lady of the Spanish Court, played a part in the destinies of the islands as mistress or wife of men who took part in the conquest of the Canaries.

Beatriz de Bobadilla

As mistress of King Ferdinand of Aragon she attracted the wrath of his wife Isabella of Castile, who took the first opportunity to get rid of her rival. Hernán Peraza the Younger, who was suspected of having murdered the conqueror of the Canaries, was pardoned on condition that he married Beatriz de Bobadilla and took her with him to Gomera. The couple were ruthless in their treatment of the native population, who reacted violently, and Hernán Peraza was killed during a rising in 1488. Thereupon Beatriz de Bobadilla entrenched herself in the Torre del Conde in San Sebastián. The Governor of the island of Gran Canaria came to her assistance, the rebellion was repressed and its ringleaders executed.

As ruler of Gomera Beatriz several times received Columbus (see entry), and when he called in at Gomera on his second voyage of discovery she greeted him with fireworks and an artillery salute. Whether she had a liaison with Columbus cannot be certainly established, but there is no doubt about her next love-affair: in 1498 she married Alonso Fernández de Lugo (see entry), conqueror of Tenerife and La Palma.

This seductive lady is still not forgotten on Gomera, and her portrait occupies a place of honour in the parador high above San Sebastián.

Christopher Columbus (in Spanish Cristóbal Colón, in Italian Cristoforo Colombo), a native of Genoa, visited the Canaries several times on his voyages of discovery.

Christopher Columbus
(1451–1506)

Columbus went to Lisbon in 1476 hoping to get assistance for his project of seeking a western route to India; then, proving

Notable Personalities

Jean de Béthencourt

Beatriz de Bobadilla

Columbus

unsuccessful, applied to Spain in 1485. It was not until 1492, however, that Ferdinand of Aragon and his wife Isabella of Castile signed an agreement with Columbus making him viceroy of any lands he discovered and granting him 10 per cent of the expected profits.

On his first voyage (1492–93) Columbus put in at Las Palmas (Gran Canaria), where he had his ships overhauled and took on supplies of water and provisions. During his stay he lived in the house which still bears his name, the Casa de Colón. At the end of August he set out for Gomera; and his logbook records that when sailing past Tenerife he observed an eruption of Mount Teide. During his stay on Gomera he met Beatriz de Bobadilla (see entry); but whether he had a liaison with her, as rumour had it, is uncertain. That there may have been some truth in the story is suggested by the fact that Columbus also spent some time on Gomera on his second (1493–95) and third (1498–1500) voyages. His visits have earned Gomera the style of "Isla Colombina".

On his fourth crossing of the Atlantic (1502–04) Columbus again took on supplies on Gran Canaria. On his return from this voyage he was a sick man, and he died in Valladolid in 1506.

Alonso Fernández de Lugo
(1456–1525)

The Andalusian nobleman Alonso Fernández de Lugo played the principal part in the conquest of the Canaries.
He entered into an agreement with Ferdinand of Aragon and Isabella of Castile under which he was given the right to grant land and water rights on the Canary Islands. For his part he was required to raise the resources for the conquest of La Palma and Tenerife.

On 1 May 1492, de Lugo, who had previously taken part in the conquest of Gran Canaria, landed on Tenerife with a thousand men; but after some initial successes he suffered an annihilating defeat in the Barranco de Acentejo. In 1492–93 he conquered the island of La Palma without difficulty, then in the autumn of 1494 he again landed on Tenerife and by 1496 had brought the whole island under his control. In the same year he founded La Laguna and made it his capital. In 1498 he married Beatriz de Bobadilla (see entry). He showed great skill in the government of the islands, but there are differing views about his character. He is sometimes seen as an adventurer who treated the native population with great harshness and whose motives for action were his debts and his greed for money.

Visitors to the Canaries will frequently come across the work of the architect, painter and sculptor César Manrique, a native of Lanzarote. The buildings and developments for which he has been responsible, including the Costa de Martiánez in Puerto de la Cruz, have left a distinctive mark on the landscape of the Canaries.

César Manrique (b. 1920)

After some early exhibitions of his work in the Canaries Manrique moved in 1945 to Madrid, where he studied at the Academy of Fine Art. Thereafter he achieved further success in the field of abstract painting, and his work was exhibited not only in Spain but in many cities in Europe, Japan and the United States. In 1965, now with an international reputation, he went to New York to take up a post in the International Institute of Art Education. In 1968 he returned to Lanzarote, where he founded the Museum of Contemporary Art.

Since then he has been concerned in numerous building projects in the Canaries, particularly on Lanzarote and Tenerife. Basing himself on native architectural traditions, he seeks to preserve the landscape as it is; architecture should be in harmony with its setting. He sees it as his principal task to save his native island of Lanzarote from over-building. In this he has been successful; there is only a single tower block on Lanzarote and the bizarre landscape of the island remains unspoiled by electricity pylons or advertising signs.

History

From 3000 B.C.

The Canaries are believed to have been settled by at least two waves of incomers. The first human type to reach the islands has more Cro-Magnon characteristics than later arrivals, who show Mediterranean features. The history of these first inhabitants (see Early Inhabitants), living almost totally isolated from the rest of the world, is obscure. There are no written records – apart from some rock inscriptions which have not been deciphered – until the Spanish conquest in the 15th c.

From 1100 B.C.

Other ancient peoples are aware of the existence of the Canary archipelago. In the course of their exploratory voyages along the West African coast the Phoenicians and later the Carthaginians visit the islands but no regular trading contacts develop.

Between 25 B.C. and A.D. 23

King Juba II of Mauretania (25 B.C.–A.D. 23) sends ships to the Canaries, which, on the evidence of Pliny the Elder, they seem to have reached.

1st c. A.D.

Pliny the Elder (A.D. 23–79) mentions the islands in his "Natural History" and gives their names, together with information about dimensions and distances which is not in accordance with the facts.

2nd c. A.D.

The Greek geographer Ptolemy (c. A.D. 100–160) shows the islands on his map of the world – the first map to give degrees of longitude. He makes the prime meridian – the end of the then known world – pass through the western tip of Hierro, the Punta de Orchilla.

End of 13th c.

The Canaries, having fallen into oblivion for many centuries, are rediscovered by European seafarers questing for slaves.

1312

The Genoese seaman Lancelot Maloisel (Lanzarotto Malocello) cruises in the Canaries and lands on the island later to be named after him, Lanzarote. He retains possession of the island until 1330.

1340–42

The Portuguese and Spaniards send ships to the Canaries, many of them from Majorca. Since they are usually heavily armed and carry horses, the objective is probably not merely trade.

1344

Pope Clement VI, as having authority over "all lands to be discovered", appoints Luís de la Cerda, a scion of the Spanish royal family, King of the Canary Islands – though this title does not imply possession of the land.

End of 14th c.

Roberto de Bracamonte succeeds Luís de la Cerda but, like him, is content with the purely theoretical title of king and makes no attempt to conquer the islands. He leaves this task to his cousin Jean de Béthencourt (1359–1425: see Notable Personalities).

1402

Together with the Spanish nobleman Gadifer de la Salle (c. 1340–1422) Jean de Béthencourt makes the first attempt to win the Canaries for the Spanish Crown. After occupying Lanzarote Béthencourt is granted the title of King of the Canary Islands. Gadifer de la Salle takes no part in further conquests after his claim to the title is rejected.

Béthencourt conquers the islands of Fuerteventura and Hierro but fails in his attempts to take Gran Canaria and La Palma. He returns to France in 1406.   1405

Béthencourt appoints his nephew Maciot de Béthencourt Viceroy of the islands. In 1415, however, on the intervention of the King, he is compelled to retire on the ground of incompetence, but sells his office successively to the Royal Envoy, Diego de Herrera, Prince Henry of Portugal and a Spanish Count, Hernán Peraza the Elder. The situation about possession of the islands thus becomes thoroughly confused, and in subsequent years ships are sent both by Spaniards and Portuguese to conquer them.   1406–15

Hernán Peraza the Elder, who hitherto has alternated between Fuerteventura, Hierro and Gomera, finally establishes his authority on Gomera and builds the famous Torre del Conde. He and his successors rule the island with ruthless disregard of the interests of the inhabitants.   1445

The Spanish Crown purchases the right of sovereignty over the islands of Fuerteventura, Lanzarote, Gomera and Hierro.   1478

The Treaty of Alcáçovas settles Spanish and Portuguese territorial claims: the Canary Islands are recognized as Spanish, and Portugal is compensated by the whole of West Africa and various offshore islands.   1479

After several unsuccessful attempts the island of Gran Canaria is finally conquered in April 1483.   1479–83

On his first voyage of discovery Columbus (in Spanish Cristóbal Colón: see Notable Personalities) puts in at Gran Canaria and then at Gomera. On his later voyages (1493, 1498 and 1502) he calls in several times at these islands and once at Hierro.   1492

Alonso Fernández de Lugo, an Andalusian noble (see Notable Personalities) lands on La Palma and establishes his authority over the whole island.   1492–93

Alonso Fernández de Lugo gradually conquers the whole of Tenerife, which has preserved its independence longer than any other of the Canary Islands. The island then, like Gran Canaria and La Palma, becomes directly subject to the Spanish Crown. Supreme authority is exercised by *capitanes generales* (captains-general), who allocate the usufruct (exploitation without ownership) of land and sell water rights.
Gomera, Hierro, Lanzarote and Fuerteventura have the status of *señorios*. The Spanish Crown has sovereignty over these islands but grants rights of possession – in effect fiefs – to nobles and ecclesiastics, subject to duties payable to the rulers of the islands and to the Spanish Crown.   1494–96

Alonso Fernández de Lugo founds the town of La Laguna as his capital and the administrative centre of Tenerife.   1496

History

16th–17th c.	The indigenous population of the Canaries – apart from those who have been sold as slaves – become gradually assimilated to the Spanish conquerors. The islands rapidly acquire economic importance through the cultivation of sugar-cane and later the production of wine.
1537	After the Spanish conquest slavery is forbidden, but the ban is frequently evaded, as is shown by a further decree by Pope Paul III making slavery a punishable offence.
1657	Britain makes several attempts to take the Canary Islands. An attack by Admiral Blake is beaten off.
1706	During the War of the Spanish Succession Admiral Jennings makes another unsuccessful attempt to conquer the islands.
1723	Santa Cruz de Tenerife displaces La Laguna as capital of Tenerife.
1778	The port of Santa Cruz de Tenerife is granted the right to trade with America.
1797	Nelson, commanding eight warships, threatens Santa Cruz. He makes a landing with 1200 men, but after the Spaniards receive reinforcements he is compelled to withdraw.
1799	In the course of his voyage to South America Alexander von Humboldt (1769–1859) spends some time on Tenerife (see Quotations).
1822	Santa Cruz de Tenerife becomes capital of the whole archipelago.
1837	The *señorio* status of Gomera, Hierro, Lanzarote and Fuerteventura is abolished.
1852	Queen Isabella II declares the Canaries a free trade zone.
End of 19th c.	The cultivation and export of bananas becomes the mainstay of the Canarian economy.
1912	The islands are granted local self-government. The Cabildos Insulares (Island Councils) are established.
1927	The Canary Islands are divided into two provinces, Santa Cruz de Tenerife (Tenerife, Gomera, Hierro and La Palma) and Las Palmas de Gran Canaria (Gran Canaria, Lanzarote and Fuerteventura).
1936	General Francisco Franco (1892–1975), commander of the military region of the Canaries, meets his senior officers in the Bosque de Tenerife to plan the military coup which leads to the Spanish Civil War (1936–39).
1971	Volcanic eruption (Volcán de Teneguía) on La Palma, the most recent eruption in the Canaries.
1975	After Franco's death Juan Carlos becomes King of Spain.
1977	On 26 March Los Rodeos Airport on Tenerife is the scene of one of the world's worst aircraft accidents, in which 577 people

are killed. Spain reacts quickly to the disaster; the Reina Sofia Airport in the south of the island, which meets the highest standards of safety, is opened only a year later. Almost all international flights now use this airport.

A new democratic constitution comes into force; Spain becomes a constitutional monarchy. 1978

The Canary Islands, together with the other sixteen autonomous regions of Spain, gets its own regional constitution and elected representative bodies. 1983

On 1 January Spain becomes a member of the EEC; there is a special agreement on the Canaries. 1986

Early Inhabitants

The name Guanches is frequently but erroneously applied to the indigenous inhabitants of the Canaries. Strictly, however, this term applies only to the inhabitants of Tenerife. The word Guanche in the old Canarian language means "son of Tenerife" (from *guan* = son, *Achinech* = Tenerife). The original population of the other islands had different names: for example the inhabitants of Hierro were called Bimbaches. In this section the early inhabitants of the Canarian as a whole are not called Guanches but ancient Canarians.

Origin

The origin of the ancient Canarians is still an enigma. The "catastrophe theory" of some early geologists, who believed that the Canaries had been separated from the African continent together with some surviving inhabitants, is no longer tenable. The first inhabitants of the islands must, therefore, have reached them by boat, although no remains of any such craft have so far been found.

It is established, however, that the ancient Canarians belonged to two different racial types. A considerable proportion were of Cro-Magnon race (named after the type site in France), with long skulls, broad faces, high foreheads and short narrow noses. The Spanish chroniclers describe the inhabitants of the Canaries as tall and broad-shouldered, with fair hair and light-coloured eyes. There was also another race, taller and slenderer, and of Mediterranean type. It is assumed, therefore, that the islands were settled by at least two waves of incomers.

Since Fuerteventura lies only some 96 km (60 miles) off the African mainland, the first settlers may have come from there. This theory finds support in the fact that there are still people living in north-west Africa who belong to the Cro-Magnon type. Moreover, with the normal currents and trade winds, a boat leaving the coast of what is now Morocco would be driven south past the Canaries. On the other hand it was much easier, in spite of the greater distance, to reach the archipelago from the Iberian Peninsula. The ancient Canarians, therefore, were not necessarily descended from the prehistoric inhabitants of north-west Africa, and there may also have been connections with the Atlantic coast of western Europe. Such evidence as we have of the culture of the ancient Canarians (megalithic petroglyphs, forms of religion, etc.) suggests possible affinities with the megalithic culture.

There remains the question of when the settlement of the Canaries took place. The ancient Canarians had no knowledge of metals, and their remains suggest that contact with other peoples must have been broken off as early as the Neolithic period. Some authorities believe that the first settlers reached the archipelago about 3000 B.C. It is unlikely that there were any major waves of immigration after 1000 B.C.

Cultural level

The ancient Canarians were herdsmen and primitive tillers of the soil. On land cleared from the forest they grew barley and wheat, and also pulses, without the aid of the plough. Their domestic animals were goats, sheep, pigs and dogs.

Dwellings

They lived mainly in caves, which suited the climatic conditions of the time. The interiors of the caves were often hewn smooth, and sometimes had thatched reed ceilings. Artificial caves were sometimes hewn from the rock. There were also occasional stone structures, particularly tombs, roofed holes in the ground and straw-covered wattle-and-daub huts.

The staple food was *gofio* – roasted barley, ground into a powder, mixed with honey and water and rolled into balls. Other important foodstuffs were goat-meat, milk and butter. Mushrooms and wild fruits were gathered in the forests. Fish and seafood must also have featured on the menu – though, lacking boats, the ancient Canarians could fish only in waters just off the coast.

Food

The clothing of the ancient Canarians was primitive. A common garment was the *tamarco*, a skin cloak made by joining goatskins with thorns from plants. The art of weaving was unknown, although there were sheep on the islands. Garments were also made of plaited palm fibres and bast.

Clothing

When the Spaniards conquered the islands in the 15th c. they had little difficulty in overcoming the inhabitants, who had only the most primitive weapons. The bow and arrow were unknown to them, and their only means of defence were stones, fire-hardened throwing-spears and wooden clubs. For hand-to-hand fighting they had thin pointed stone blades, so sharp that they could also be used for cutting up objects. They had no metal tools or weapons, and lacked even the ground stone axes of the Neolithic period.

Tools and weapons

That the ancient Canarians, in spite of these living conditions, were not entirely primitive cave-men is shown by their social structure. There were three classes of society – the king and his family, the nobles and the rest of the population. There seems to have been no clear distinction between the second and third groups. Nobility was not hereditary but could be attained by personal qualities, and noble status had to be confirmed by the priests. On the individual islands there were independent tribal territories under the overlordship of the king; on Tenerife there was apparently a kind of double kingship.
Inheritance was in the female line, but it was not a matriarchal society. A woman could not herself exercise royal authority, but her husband was authorized by her election to rule. In practice the system of inheritance in the female line gave women a high status in society.
There is some evidence that women played a major part in religious rites. On Fuerteventura two women are said to have taken the leading roles in legal and religious matters.

Social structure

The ancient Canarians believed in a single all-powerful higher being. On the island of Tenerife it was the god Abora. He had an adversary in Guayote, who was confined in the crater of Mount Teide and punished the misdeeds of men with volcanic eruptions. An important part was played in the religious practices of the Canarians by sacred mountains and cave sanctuaries, where animal sacrifices and libations were made to the god.

Religion

To the ancient Canarians the world of the dead was closely bound up with the world of the living. Dwellings and burial-

Burial practices

33

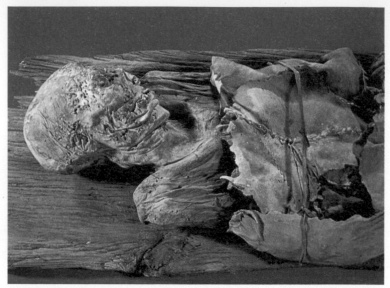

An ancient Canarian mummy

places cannot always be clearly distinguished from one another, for both natural and man-made caves were used either for living in or for burial. Only on the island of Gran Canaria have burial mounds been found. The bodies of the higher classes of the population were mummified by being annointed with goat's-milk butter and preserved by the application of heat and smoke. The brain was never removed; nor, normally, the entrails. This, compared with Egyptian methods, was a very primitive form of mummification, and in spite of the dry climate the mummies did not last long without decomposing. Evidently the caves traditionally used for burial were repeatedly reoccupied. The mummies found in such caves and now displayed in the museums of Santa Cruz de Tenerife and Las Palmas de Gran Canaria are none of them very old.

Language

Only scanty remnants of the language of the ancient Canarians have survived into our day, mainly in the form of place-names. It has been suggested, on the basis of this evidence, that the Canarian tongue was related to the language of the Berbers. It may be, however, that Berber elements entered the language at some later date. The various islands had different dialects, though basic words were common to them all. It is uncertain whether the whistling language known as *el silbo* (see "A to Z", Gomera) was peculiar to the island of Gomera or was also used on Tenerife.

When the Spaniards conquered the Canaries the native population had no written script. Many rock inscriptions have been found on the islands, some quite recently. The first such inscriptions were discovered in 1867 on La Palma (Cueva

Belmaco); then in 1870 there was found on Hierro (Los Letreros) a rock face with inscriptions of different periods – a kind of pictographic script which conveyed only ideas and concepts, a series of characters resembling an alphabetic script and various forms transitional between the two. On Gran Canaria there are rock-cut spirals and concentric circles (megalithic petroglyphs); only on Tenerife and Gomera has nothing comparable been found. The scripts have not so far been deciphered, and it is doubtful whether they ever will be, for souvenir-hunters have broken off much of the rock faces bearing the inscriptions. It is also uncertain whether the inscriptions were the work of the Canarians themselves or of occasional visitors.

Some handsome pieces of pottery, made without the use of a wheel, have survived from the pre-Hispanic period. Many of them have hollow handles which could also be used as spouts. They are mostly plain and undecorated, but some are patterned with nicks or notches. The forms vary from island to island: thus on La Palma stamped or impressed decoration was used, and on Gran Canaria the decoration was particularly elaborate.

Art

Mention should also be made here of the *pintaderas* – seals in a great variety of patterns, usually made of pottery, rarely of wood. They were presumably used to mark objects with the owner's name. No two *pintaderas* with the same pattern have so far been found.

There were also figures of idols, presumably used in various cult ceremonies, which almost without exception have survived only in fragments. The only one of any artistic quality is the "Idol of Tara", perhaps the most celebrated relic of ancient Canarian culture, which was found on Gran Canaria. This clay figure with grotesquely fat limbs is thought to be female, though there are no indications of breasts.

In total there are only scanty remnants of ancient Canarian art, all of modest artistic pretensions.

In general the remains of ancient Canarian culture are characterized by archaic simplicity; but there are also elements which appear to belong to a higher cultural level. Thus wheat and barley were ground on a circular hand-mill of a type found in antiquity throughout the Mediterranean region, in which the grain was introduced through a funnel-like opening in the upper stone. Since this piece of relatively advanced technology is out of line with other ancient Canarian remains it is supposed that it was brought to the islands by other peoples. Similarly the rock-cut inscriptions found on the islands may have been left by foreign visitors. It is certainly the case that the Canarians had sporadic contacts with other peoples before the coming of the Spaniards: for example Roman amphorae or fragments of amphorae have been found off the coasts of the Canaries.

Influences of other cultures

After the Spanish conquest the culture of the ancient Canarians, their language and way of life, fell completely into oblivion. In consequence it was long believed that the conquerers had ruthlessly exterminated the native population. There is no doubt that large numbers of Canarians were enslaved and shipped away from the islands and that the

Hispanization of the Canarians

Stone hand-mill, perhaps brought to the Canaries by a foreign visitor

population was decimated in the fighting with the invaders. Many, however, survived, and anthropological study has revealed the persistence of ancient Canarian racial characteristics in the present-day population of the Canaries. There must, therefore, have been a very rapid mingling of the two races after the Spanish conquest. The ancient Canarians became rapidly assimilated and adopted the way of the life of the Spaniards – not surprisingly, for Spanish culture was much superior to their own.

Quotations

But to thee is assigned, O beloved of Zeus, Menelaus,
Not the destiny of death in Argos, mother of horses;
But the gods will lead thee one day to the end of the earth,
To the Elysian fields, where the dark-skinned Rhadamanthys
Dwells, and men are blessed with an ever tranquil life.
There is no snow, no winter storm, no pouring rain;
And there is ever heard the murmur of the softly-breathing West,
Which Ocean sends to bring men gentle coolness.

Homer
"Odyssey"
(8th c. B.C.)

(Whether the "Elysian fields" described by Homer are to be identified with the Canary Islands is an open question.)

There are two islands, separated from one another by a narrow strait, ten thousand stadia from Africa; they are called the Isles of the Blessed. Seldom watered by moderate showers of rain, most commonly by gentle dew-bringing winds, they offer not only a good rich soil to be tilled and planted but also wild fruits sufficient in quantity and flavour to nourish an idle people without work or effort.

Plutarch
"Life of Sertorius"
(1st–2nd c. A.D.)

These islands enjoy a fortunate climate in consequence of the mingling and the barely perceptible change of the seasons; for the north and east winds blowing from our region of the earth are dispersed and die down when they emerge into this expanse of infinite space, and the sea winds from the south and west sometimes bring in moderate rain from the sea, but for the most part caress the islands with their gentle breath and make them fertile. And so there has been disseminated even among the barbarians the firm belief that these are the Elysian fields, the dwelling-place of the blessed, of which Homer sang.

9 August 1492

As we were passing Tenerife we observed an eruption of the volcano. The smoke and flames, the glowing masses of lava, the muffled roaring from the earth's interior caused panic among the crew. An evil omen, they thought, it must surely be. I told them about Etna and other volcanoes, but found only deaf ears. They believed that the volcano had erupted because we had undertaken this voyage. This caused me worry enough, but I was still more disturbed by the news brought by a ship coming from Ferro [Hierro]. It reported that three Portuguese caravels were cruising in the vicinity, with orders to take me prisoner and so put an end to my enterprise.

Christopher Columbus
"Logbook"
(1492)

The way from La Rábida to Córdoba is long, from Palos to Lisbon still longer; and yet the King of Portugal already knew that I had put to sea. He no longer needs me now that Diaz has found the eastern route to India, and so he wants to bar the western route to me. If I succeed – and I shall succeed – in winning the sea and reaching territories where no other vessels dare to go João's caravels will return to Lisbon empty handed. Time, which has always run too fast for me, is now running too slowly. It will take another three weeks to make the "Pinta" seaworthy.

Quotations

In these Canary Islands there were three different methods of fighting, with three different kinds of weapon: the two which have already been mentioned and a third, the thin stones called *tavas* which they used for letting blood. These they employ to wound one another in hand-to-hand fighting.

When two Canarians challenged one another to a fight they made their way to the spot used for this purpose, a small area of higher ground with a flat stone on each side, just big enough for a man to stand on. Each of them stood on his stone with three pebbles to throw at his opponent and wound him, and with the cudgels called *magodo* and *amodeghe*. They began by throwing the stones at each other, dexterously avoiding them without moving their feet. Then they stepped off their stones and had at each other with the cudgels, each striving to gain an advantage over the other, just as it is with us; and when they came hand to hand they wounded one another with the three sharp stones which they held between the fingers of the left hand. Then when one of the two was ready to admit defeat he cried out in a loud voice *"Gamá, gamá"*, which in our language means "Enough, enough!". Thereupon the victor ceased to fight and the two men became friends. Before challenging one another to fight they had first obtained permission from a chieftain called a *sambor* and this permission had been confirmed by a *faicagh* (priest). Both the chieftain and the priest, as well as the relatives of the two men, were present at the fight.

To speake somewhat of these Ilands, being called in olde time Insulae Fortunatae, by the meanes of the flourishing thereof, the fruitfullnesse of them doeth surely exceed farre all other that I have heard of: for they make wine better than any in Spaine, they have grapes of such bignesse, that they may bee compared to damsons, and taste inferiour to none: for sugar, suckets, rasins of the Sunne, and many other fruits, abundance: for rosine and rawe silke, there is great store, they want neither corne, pullets, cattell, nor yet wilde foule: they have many camels also which being young are eaten of the people for victuals, and being olde, they are used for caryage of necessaries.

Tenerife, situated as it were at the gateway of the tropics and yet only a few days' sail from Spain, already displays much of the splendour with which nature has endowed the lands between the tropics. . . . Anyone who has a feeling for the beauty of nature will find on this delightful island a remedy even more powerful than the climate. No place in the world seems to me more likely than Tenerife and Madeira to banish melancholy and restore peace to a troubled spirit. . . . The coast is fringed with date-palms and coconut trees; higher up banana plants stand out from dragon trees, whose stem is quite properly likened to the body of a snake. The hillsides are planted with vines clinging to tall trellises. Blossom-covered orange trees, myrtles and cypresses surround chapels which piety has erected on isolated hills. Everywhere the fields are enclosed by hedges of agave and cactus. Countless cryptogams, particularly ferns, clothe the walls, which are kept moist by small springs of clear water. In winter, when the volcano is covered with ice and snow, an eternal spring prevails here. In summer, towards evening, the sea wind brings agreeable coolness.

Ascent of Teide

We settled down on the outermost rim of the crater and looked first to the north-west, where the coasts are decked with villages and hamlets. The mist at our feet, continually driven this way and that by the wind, offered us an ever-changing spectacle. A level layer of clouds between us and the lower regions of the island was pierced here and there by the little currents of air which the earth's surface, warmed by the sun, sent up to us. The harbour of Orotava, the vessels anchored in it, the gardens and vineyards round the town were visible through an opening which seemed to become bigger every moment. From these lonely regions we looked down into an inhabited world, relishing the sharp contrast between the barren flanks of the peak, its steep slopes covered with volcanic detritus, its plantless plateau and the smiling aspect of the cultivated land; we saw how the vegetation was distributed into zones according to temperature, declining with increasing height. Below the summit lichens are beginning to clothe the shining flows of lava. A violet (*Viola cheiranthifolia*), closely related to *Viola decumbens*, grows at heights of up to 3390 metres (11,120 ft) on the slopes of the volcano. *Retama* bushes, covered with flowers, grow in the little valleys carved out by rainwater and blocked by the lateral eruptions. Below the *retama* follows the region of the ferns, which in turn are followed by the tree heaths. Forests of laurels, *rhamnus* and strawberry trees lie between the heaths and the area planted with vines and fruit trees. A rich green carpet extends from the level of the brooms and the zone of Alpine plants to the groups of date-palms and bananas, against whose feet the ocean seems to wash.

That from the summit of the peak the little villages, the vineyards and gardens on the coast appear so near is largely due to the extraordinary transparency of the air. In spite of the considerable distance we could not only make out the houses, the trunks of the trees, the rigging of the ships; we could also see the rich flora of the plains gleaming in the liveliest colours. The splendour of the landscape in the tropics is mainly due to this transparency; it enhances the brilliant colours of the plants and increases the magical effect of their harmonies and their contrasts.

In vain we prolonged our stay on the summit, waiting for the moment when we should be able to see the whole archipelago of the Blessed Islands. We saw at our feet Palma, Gomera and Grand Canary, but soon the hills of Lanzarote, which at sunrise had been clear, were again shrouded in dense mist.

Sunrise on the 11th March was an unforgettable moment. Dark masses of cloud all round, and below them, to the left, the broad shape of Hierro; then a blood-red spot, which gradually dissolved into an ethereal light purple and greenish blue; the fairy-tale island of Palma lay before us, framed in clouds, and the pretty little town of Santa Cruz de la Palma looked up invitingly, climbing the steep slopes at the exact point where a number of deep *barrancos* [gorges] come together and debouch into the sea. Above it, at a majestic height, the ridges of the Cumbre, covered everywhere with dark, almost tropical green, all the hills fringed with dense forests of Canary pine. From the ridges descended innumerable *barrancos*, like the sharp, narrow pleats in a garment.

And now, all of a sudden, the sun illuminated the magical

Hermann Christ
Swiss botanist
"Spring Journey
to the Canaries"
(1886)

scene; the town gleamed in the purest white, the shadows in the gorges turned blue, the green was bordered with glints of emerald. The island fell away below us in a mighty sweep, its longer side extending towards the south. Hundreds of houses spangled the deep green landscape, like white pearls scattered with a lavish hand. . . . What coastal scenery! A steep *barranco* passed close to the houses of the town as it plunged towards the sea; on its left-hand wall was a horn-shaped crag resembling the Gütschen on Lake Uri; in the water lay a mass of coal-black lava with something of the form of a rose, with the waves washing over it; in the rock face just above it was a cave containing mummies of the indigenous population; a boldly engineered road wound its way up the cliff, the new Carretera de la Banda leading to the west side of the island, at the mouth of the caldera; to the right the dainty white houses of the little town climbed high up the hillside, combining tropical architecture with Dutch cleanliness; the lines of houses were agreeably interrupted by orange groves, palms, banks of red and white roses, the delicate white feather-like blossoms of the West Indian rose-apple tree, the blood-red carpets of the bougainvillaeas; the scene was completed by a number of church towers of dark-coloured lava and – not to be forgotten – an elegant new arena for cockfights, the sport of the people of Palma.

I called on the agent of the steamship line, who was kindly getting a guide for me. The tradespeople of Santa Cruz de la Palma live in tall, handsome, well-furnished houses; instead of the poverty or neglect which we might expect to encounter on this remote, forgotten island, we find comfort, meticulous cleanliness, light and air, such as are not always to be met with even in favoured regions in the advanced countries of Europe. And how charming is this street! Looking down on it is a deep blue sky; shafts of golden light fall on the lava paving-slabs, transfiguring them; the green of the delicately carved openwork shutters which usually take the place of windows stands out sharply against the white of the walls; as almost everywhere in the Canaries, the shutters have a small flap, opening from the bottom, which enables the occupants of the house to look out into the street whenever they feel inclined. And these flaps are busily in action when the Englishman strides along the lava paving in his Indian sun-helmet – a complete novelty here. Everywhere are cheerful, happy, pretty faces, laughing out loud and joking about the stiff foreigner, showing the whitest teeth and the blackest and most brilliant eyes.

Suggested Itineraries

In this section we suggest a series of itineraries on Tenerife. For suggested itineraries on Gomera, Hierro and La Palma see the entries on these islands in the "A to Z" section of this guide.

Apart from the circuit of the island (Route 1) the itineraries are given in alternative forms, one starting from Puerto de la Cruz, the other from Los Cristianos (or Playa de las Américas). The general course of the itinerary can be seen from the marginal references.

The distances given do not include detours.

Places which are the subject of a separate entry in the "A to Z" section are printed in bold type. Descriptions of other places can be found by reference to the Index.

Route 1: Circuit of the island (c. 220 km (140 miles))

Puerto de la Cruz is taken as the starting-point of this itinerary, but it is of course possible to begin from any place on the route. In general, however, it is better to begin with the west of the island, where the roads are not so good and visibility is important. A tour of Santa Cruz de Tenerife or La Laguna, on the other hand, is still of interest in the evening, and thereafter the northern and southern motorways make it easy to get back to any particular resort.

If only a single day can be devoted to this itinerary this will allow only a very short time in any of the places on the route and will give only a first brief impression of the beauty and interest that Tenerife has to offer.

Leave **Puerto de la Cruz**, going east. In 4 km (2½ miles) we join the N820 and turn west for 1 km (¾ mile) to the turning for **La Orotava**, where many handsome old houses with typical Canarian balconies can be seen. From the Plaza de la Constitución in the centre of the town there is a fine view of the **Valle de la Orotava**. From the town centre a narrow road passes through the village of La Perdoma to **Los Realejos**. Continuing through the long straggling town to Realejo Bajo, we rejoin the N820, here running parallel to the coast. The route then continues west to **San Juan de la Rambla** and **Icod**, where the dragon tree, the oldest and finest on Tenerife, is a great attraction for every visitor. 6 km (3½ miles) beyond this on the coast road lies **Garachico** with its charming old town centre. From the end of the town a road winds its way up to Tanque, a short distance beyond which we rejoin the N820. Plenty of time must be allowed for the next part of the route, with the road turning and twisting through the lonely hill country. The next place of any size is Santiago del Teide, a base for walks and climbs in the **Teno Hills** to the west. Some 5 km (3 miles) beyond Santiago del Teide, at Tamaimo, the road forks. If time permits the road which leads south to **Puerto de Santiago** should be taken. The imposing cliffs of Los Gigantes soon come in sight. After a brief detour to the attractive holiday development of Los Gigantes, north of Puerto de Santiago, the

Puerto de la Cruz

La Orotava

Los Realejos

Icod

Garachico

Santiago del Teide

Puerto de Santiago

Suggested Itineraries

Alcalá	route continues along the coast through Alcalá and San Juan
Adeje	to **Adeje** (30 km (18½ miles) from Tamaimo).

Short cut via Guía de Isora · A shorter (25 km (15½ miles)) and quicker route from Tamaimo to Adeje runs inland via Guía de Isora and Tejina. From Adeje, an unspoiled little town, the large tourist centres in the south of Tenerife, **Playa de las Américas** and **Los Cristianos**, can be rapidly reached on the N822. From Los Cristianos a good road leads east to the Reina Sofia (Tenerife Sur) Airport. Beyond the airport, which handles almost all the island's international traffic, the route continues on the four-lane Autopista del Sur. It is 45 km (28 miles) to the exit for **Candelaria**, the most important place of pilgrimage in the Canaries. 16 km (10 miles) beyond this on the motorway lies the island's capital, **Santa Cruz**.

Los Cristianos

Reina Sofia Airport

Candelaria

Santa Cruz

Visitors who prefer to bypass this busy city should turn into the Autopista del Norte shortly before Santa Cruz and continue to **La Laguna**, the only university town in the Canaries, a quiet little place which has preserved its original character and is almost untouched by the tourist trade. The return from here to Puerto de la Cruz is on the Autopista del Norte (*c.* 35 km (22 miles)).

La Laguna

Puerto de la Cruz

Route 2: Valle de la Orotava and Caldera de las Cañadas

A trip to the Orotava Valley and the Caldera de las Cañadas is one of the most unforgettable impressions of a visit to Tenerife,

▼ *The large holiday resort of Los Christianos, in the south of Tenerife*

on a route which traverses all the island's various vegetation zones.

To get the best views of Mount Teide it is essential to start early in the morning. Later in the day the peak is almost always shrouded in dense clouds.

2A: from Puerto de la Cruz (c. 180 km (112 miles))

From **Puerto de la Cruz** take one of the many link roads running south to **La Orotava**, from which the N821 climbs up to the Caldera de las Cañadas. At first the road traverses luxuriant banana plantations, which soon give place to vineyards, orchards and fields of vegetables. At Aguamansa (alt. 1000 m (3300 ft)) the vegetation changes again to dense forests of laurels, pines and tree heaths.

Puerto de la Cruz
La Orotava

1 km (¾ mile) beyond the Aguamansa car park a side road branches off on the left to the Caldera, a small subsidiary crater. It is a 10 minutes' walk round the crater, and a rather longer walk to Los Órganos (The Organ-Pipes), curiously shaped columns of lava rock.

Walk to the Caldera
and Los Órganos

Higher up is the Mirador Marguerite, another good starting-point for walks.

The road leads past the Montaña Roja (1800 m (5900 ft)) and at El Portillo (2020 m (6630 ft)), the "gateway" to the **Caldera de las Cañadas**, meets the road from La Laguna. Continuing on the N821, we come, soon after El Portillo, to the Visitor Centre of the **Parque Nacional del Teide**.

El Portillo

We are now in the midst of a lunar landscape. The vegetation is confined to low ground-covering plants, with occasional patches of scrub. The road now climbs only very gently, surrounded by rocks shimmering in an endless variety of colour. At the Montaña Blanca a plan of the route to the summit of **Teide** is displayed. 1·5 km (1 mile) beyond this a road goes off on the right to the lower station of the cableway up the Pico de Teide. Just 4 km (2½ miles) beyond the cableway station, on the right, is a large picnic area, and a few hundred metres beyond this a road on the left leads to the Parador Nacional de las Cañadas and on the right to Los Roques, perhaps the most imposing rock formation on Tenerife. From the viewpoint at Los Roques there is a prospect of the Llano de Ucanca, an extensive plain which the road soon afterwards traverses.

Boca de Tauce

At the Boca de Tauce (2046 m (6713 ft)) we leave the Caldera de las Cañadas and continue south-east on the N821, passing through dense forest. Near km 58 is the *zona recreativa* of Las Lajas, with a restaurant and barbecue facilities which are popular with local people at week-ends.

Detour to Paisaje Lunar

Shortly before Vilaflor (after km 65) a road diverges on the left to the Campamento Madre del Agua, from which it is possible to walk to the Paisaje Lunar (Lunar Landscape).

Vilaflor

The forest zone ends at **Vilaflor**, and the land below the village is intensively cultivated. The fields are enclosed by lines of loosely piled stones. From the far end of Vilaflor we follow the road to Granadilla de Abona, which is more interesting than the road via Arona. It soon comes to the Cruz de Tea, from which there is a fine view of the country to the south. Shortly before **Granadilla de Abona** the N821 cuts across the N822, running approximately from east to west.

Short cut

Continuing south, we come in 8 km (5 miles) to an access road to the Autopista del Sur. This motorway and the Autopista del Norte offer a quick route to the north of the island (*c.* 100 km (65 miles) to Puerto de la Cruz).

Carretera del Sur

Visitors who do not know the south of the island should drive at least some distance north-east from Granadilla de Abona on the N322, the Carretera del Sur. To the left of the road are bare ridges of hill, to the right the blue sea shimmers far below. Although there is little rain in this area the land is intensively cultivated in small, often terraced, fields. The road passes through **Arico**, **Fasnia**, **Güimar** and **Arafo**, which have no particular features of interest; and visitors who have seen enough scenery and are tired of the never-ending bends in the road can join the motorway which leads via **Santa Cruz**, **La Laguna** and **Tacoronte** to Puerto de la Cruz.

Santa Cruz
Puerto de la Cruz

2B: from Los Cristianos or Playa de las Américas (*c.* 190 km (120 miles))

Los Cristianos

The quickest way to the Caldera de las Cañadas from the south of Tenerife is via **Arona** and **Vilaflor**.

The route via San Miguel, however, is scenically much more varied. For this route leave **Los Cristianos** on the N822, which runs north-east and after passing the beautifully situated bungalow settlement of Chayofa comes in 13 km (8 miles) to

Chayofa

the Mirador de la Centinela (612 m (2008 ft)), from which there is an incomparable view of the volcanic landscape of southern Tenerife. Continuing on the N822, we pass through San Miguel and in another 5 km (3 miles) turn left into the N821. From here we follow Route 2A via Vilaflor, Boca de Tauce, the **Caldera de las Cañadas** and the **Valle de la Orotava**, in the reverse direction. 5 km (3 miles) north of **La Orotava** is the largest tourist centre in the north of the island, **Puerto de la Cruz**, where the opportunity of a walk round the town and along the beautiful seafront promenade should not be missed. The return to Los Cristianos or Playa de las Américas (*c.* 105 km (65 miles)) is by way of the northern and southern motorways.

San Miguel
Vilaflor
Caldera de las Cañadas
La Orotava

Puerto de la Cruz

Los Cristianos

Route 3: To the Caldera de las Cañadas on the Carretera Dorsal

The route to the Caldera de las Cañadas on the Carretera Dorsal (Ridgeway: a fast road) from La Laguna passes through very different scenery from the road through the Valle de la Orotava. On this route, too, an early start is advisable so as to get there before the clouds form.

3A: from Puerto de la Cruz (*c.* 170 km (105 miles))

From **Puerto de la Cruz** the quickest route to **La Laguna** is on the Autopista del Norte (*c.* 30 km (19 miles)). At La Laguna begins the Carretera Dorsal (N824), which was completed in the early 1940s. At first it traverses an intensively cultivated

Puerto de la Cruz
La Laguna

Seafront promenade, Puerto de la Cruz

45

La Esperanza

area, but above the village of La Esperanza it comes to the **Bosque de la Esperanza**, an expanse of dense forest. 2 km (1¼ miles) beyond La Esperanza a side road on the left leads to the memorial at Las Raíces, where General Franco assembled the officers of the Tenerife Garrison to plan his military coup on the Spanish mainland.

The N824 climbs up along the ridge of hills which separates the northern and southern halves of the island, passing numerous viewpoints, among the finest of which are the Mirador Pico de las Flores, the Mirador de las Cumbres and the Mirador Morro del Gaitero.

About km 32 a road goes off on the left to the Observatorio Meteorológico on Mount Izaña (2385 m (7825 ft)). 2 km (1¼ miles) farther on another road on the left leads to the Observatorio Astronómico del Teide (opened 1985), a European Community project for the exploration of space.

El Portillo

At El Portillo the Carretera Dorsal joins the N821, which we now follow into the **Caldera de las Cañadas**. Soon after the junction is the Visitor Centre of the **Parque Nacional del Teide**. The road traverses the extraordinary crater landscape round Mount Teide, passes the shimmering white Montaña Blanca (2750 m (9020 ft)), the station of the Teide cableway and Los Roques, and continues over the Llano de Ucanca.

Boca de Tauce

At Boca de Tauce (2046 m (6713 ft)) there is a choice of routes. We can either follow the route described in Route 2A or leave the N821 and continue on the N823, which runs north-west along the slopes of Mount Teide.

Tamaimo
Santiago del Teide

The N823 at first continues through the bare crater landscape and then runs through forest. In just under 30 km (19 miles) it reaches Tamaimo, where it joins the N820. We continue north on the N820 to Santiago del Teide, passing the foothills of the **Teno Hills**.

Garachico
Icod
Puerto de la Cruz

The road now descends, with endless bends. Soon after the hamlet at the Cruz Grande a narrow road branches off on the left and leads via the village of Tanque to the attractive little town of **Garachico**, from which we follow the coast road eastward via **Icod**, **San Juan de la Rambla** and **Los Realejos** to Puerto de la Cruz.

3B: from Los Cristianos or Playa de las Américas (*c.* 195 km (120 miles))

Los Cristianos
La Laguna

From Los Cristianos the route is by way of the southern or the northern motorway to **La Laguna** (80 km (50 miles)) and from there, as described in Route 3A, up through the **Bosque de la Esperanza** to the **Caldera de las Cañadas**, which is reached at El Portillo. From there to the Boca de Tauce the route is as in Route 3A.

El Portillo
Boca de Tauce

Chio
Adeje, Los Cristianos

From the Boca de Tauce visitors who do not know the Vilaflor road should follow Route 2B. Otherwise the route continues north-west on the N823: 25 km (15 miles) from the Boca de Tauce turn left for the village of Chio and then return via **Guía de Isora** and **Adeje** to Los Cristianos.

Coastal scenery in north-western Tenerife

Route 4: The Anaga Hills

This route traverses country which is still largely unspoiled, but the scenery can be appreciated only in good weather; when the Anaga Hills are shrouded in dense cloud much of their beauty is lost.

4A: from Puerto de la Cruz (*c.* 120 km (75 miles))

From Puerto de la Cruz take the Autopista del Norte to **Santa Cruz** (35 km (22 miles)). The route then turns north-east past the port to the fishing village of **San Andrés**. From there we continue on the coast road for a few hundred metres to see the palm-fringed beach of Las Teresitas, and then return to the turning for the **Montañas de Anaga**. The road winds its way up into the hills, past little peasant houses clinging to the hillsides and herds of goats clambering about among the rocks. As the road climbs the country becomes steadily greener. Finally it reaches the crest and the viewpoint of El Bailadero (9 km (5½ miles) from San Andrés), from which in good weather there are magnificent views in all directions.

Puerto de la Cruz
Santa Cruz
San Andrés

El Bailadero

From El Bailadero a detour (14 km (8½ miles) there and back) can be made to the romantically situated village of Taganana, lower down to the north, continuing to the coast at Almáciga (good bathing near by).

Detour to Taganana

From El Bailadero the route continues west along the crest of the Anaga Hills. It passes through the dense Las Mercedes

47

Forest, with many glimpses, through the trees, of the magnificent hill scenery. The best panoramic view is from the
Mirador Pico del Inglés. The laurel forest extends down to the

Las Mercedes
village of Las Mercedes, from which there are two roads to La
Laguna. Taking the road to the right, we come to the village of
Las Canteras, where we turn into the road which runs north-
west to Tegueste and Tejina over the La Laguna Plateau. This
is a densely settled area in which every little plot of land is under

Tejina
cultivation; a well-known wine is produced here. At Tejina the
road forks.

Detour to Bajamar
The road to the right leads to the quiet little bathing resorts of
Bajamar and Punta del Hidalgo (16 km (10 miles) there and
back).

Valle de Guerra
From Tejina the route continues through the Valle de Guerra,
with the village of the same name. The valley gets its name from
the battles fought here between the Guanches and the
Spaniards.

Detour to Mesa del Mar
2 km (1¼ miles) beyond the village of Valle de Guerra a narrow
and winding road branches off to the attractive holiday
development of Mesa del Mar (4 km (2½ miles) there and back).
The route continues to the typical little Canarian town of

Tacoronte
Tacoronte, 2 km (1¼ miles) south of which is the beautiful hill
forest of Agua García (pleasant walking). From here we take
not the Autopista del Norte but the old main road, the N820,

La Matanza de Acentejo
which traverses the village of La Matanza de Acentejo, where
the Spaniards were decisively defeated by the Guanches. The
name of the next village, La Victoria de Acentejo, recalls the
final Spanish victory (1495). The last place of any size before

Santa Úrsula
Puerto de la Cruz is Santa Úrsula, in an area which produces
wine, fruit, vegetables and flowers.

From here the N820 continues through luxuriant banana

Puerto de la Cruz
plantations and soon comes to the great tourist centre of Puerto
de la Cruz.

4B: from Los Cristianos or Playa de las Américas (c. 190 km (120 miles))

Los Cristianos
From Los Cristianos the Autopista del Sur offers a fast road to
Santa Cruz
Santa Cruz (c. 70 km (45 miles)), from which the route
continues through the **Montañas de Anaga** (Anaga Hills), as
San Andrés
described in Route 4A, via **San Andrés**, El Bailadero, Las
Tacoronte
Mercedes and Tejina to **Tacoronte**. Since the road from here
to Puerto de la Cruz offers nothing particularly new, the best
plan is to return to Los Cristianos from Tacoronte. Following
the signposts to Agua García, we continue south-east from
La Esperanza
there to La Esperanza, where we cross the Carretera Dorsal
(N824). Then, passing through a number of small places
Sobradillo
including Sobradillo, we join the N822 at Caserío Taco. 2 km
(1¼ miles) south on this road is the access to the Autopista del
Los Cristianos
Sur, which brings us rapidly back to our starting-point.

Route 5: The Teno Hills

This short tour takes in some of the most beautiful little towns
and villages on Tenerife and passes through the lonely Teno

Hills. Since many of the roads are not good a full day should be allowed for the tour, particularly if the detour to the Punta de Teno is included.

5A: from Puerto de la Cruz (*c.* 105 km (65 miles))

The road which goes south-east from **Puerto de la Cruz** comes in 4 km (2½ miles) to the N820, which is followed westward to the turning for **La Orotava**. Attractive in itself, the town also offers a beautiful view of the famous **Valle de la Orotava**.

Puerto de la Cruz

La Orotava

We leave La Orotava on the road which leads west to La Perdoma through one of the most fertile and most densely settled areas on the island, bordered by luxuriant banana plantations. 7 km (4½ miles) from La Orotava is Realejo Alto, part of the double town of **Los Realejos**, with the oldest church on Tenerife. From here the road follows a winding course via the villages of Tigaiga and Icod el Alto to La Guancha, where there is a craft school. 7 km (4½ miles) beyond La Guancha the road joins the N820, which we follow to **Icod**.

La Perdoma

Realejo Alto

La Guancha

Icod

After seeing the famous dragon tree we continue on the N820 to the Mirador de San Juan del Reparo (6 km (4 miles) from Icod), from which there is a view of the beautiful country round Garachico.

The road now climbs, with many windings and sharp bends, to the Erjos Pass (1117 m (3665 ft)), on the boundary between two climatic zones.

The route continues through a barren landscape to Santiago del Teide, where a road branches off to the mountain village of Masca in the **Teno Hills**. Until a few years ago the remote villages in this area could be reached only on mule-tracks: there is now a motor road from the romantically situated village of Masca via Las Portelas and El Palmar to **Buenavista** del Norte.

Santiago del Teide

Masca

Las Portelas, Buenavista

From here there is the possibility of a charming detour with impressive views of the north-west coast of Tenerife, to the Punta de Teno, the most westerly point on the island. Since the asphalt road comes to an end soon after Buenavista, 40–60 minutes should be allowed for the trip there and back (20 km (12½ miles)).

Detour to Punta de Teno

From Buenavista the route continues to **Los Silos** and **Garachico** (picturesque old town centre). 6 km (4 miles) beyond Garachico a road goes off on the left to San Marcos, a fishing village with a number of restaurants on the sea front.

Garachico
San Marcos

We now return to the junction with the N820, which runs parallel with the coast to **San Juan de la Rambla** and Realejo Bajo. Soon after Realejo Bajo we leave the N820 and turn left for the holiday development of La Romántica, from which it is a short distance, past innumerable hotels and apartment blocks, to the centre of Puerto de la Cruz.

San Juan de la Rambla

La Romántica

Puerto de la Cruz

5B: from Los Cristianos or Playa de las Américas (130 km (80 miles))

Los Cristianos
Adeje
Chio
Santiago del Teide

Masca
Buenavista, Garachico

From Los Cristianos the quickest approach to the Teno Hills is the N822, which passes the pretty little town of **Adeje** to **Guía de Isora** and Chio. Soon after Chio we leave the main road and continue via Arguayo to Santiago del Teide. From there we follow the route described in Route 5A through the **Teno Hills** to Masca and from there via **Buenavista** del Norte to **Garachico**.

Santiago del Teide

Puerto de Santiago

At the entrance to Garachico a road branches off to Tanque and 1·5 km (1 mile) beyond the village joins the N820, which we follow south to Santiago del Teide. At Tamaimo we take the road to the right, which soon brings us to **Puerto de Santiago**, with the nearby cliffs of Los Gigantes. The road now continues south, close to the coast, traversing a barren landscape. Agriculture (particularly tomato-growing) is possible here only with the help of irrigation.

San Juan

After passing through Alcalá we come to the little fishing port of San Juan. Beyond San Juan are numerous market gardens and cactus farms offering plants for sale. The landscape gradually becomes even more featureless. The road runs past many half-finished hotel buildings; the only green to relieve the monotony is provided by banana plantations.

Callao Salvaje

La Caleta

A short detour leads to the Callao Salvaje holiday development, with a number of hotels and tourist facilities. 3·5 km (2 miles) beyond Callao Salvaje we take a little road on the right which descends to the fishing village of La Caleta, where the road

A barren landscape in the south of Tenerife

ends at the sea. From here we continue south, directly on the coast. Soon after La Caleta, on the right of the road, is the Ermita de San Sebastián, with an imposing exterior and a plain and undecorated interior.

A few kilometres beyond the chapel we rejoin the N822, which soon brings us back to Los Cristianos.   Los Cristianos

Sights from A to Z

Adeje D7

Altitude: 250 m (820 ft)
Population (district): 12,000

Adeje, situated in south-western Tenerife, only a few kilometres north of Playa de las Américas and Los Cristianos (see entries), is the chief town in the district of the same name. It is predominantly a farming community, concentrating particularly on the growing of tomatoes and bananas.

Most visitors come to Adeje to make an excursion to the Barranco del Infierno.

Adeje is a quiet little town, its main street lined by white houses and planted with Indian laurels. There are a number of cafeterias.

In the main street stands the interesting Iglesia de Santa Úrsula, a two-aisled church dating from the 17th and 18th c. with a beautiful painted coffered ceiling. Above the apse are two galleries formerly reserved for noble families, with grilles to preserve the occupants from prying eyes.

A side street which leads up by the church comes in a few hundred metres to the Casa Fuerte, a fortified mansion (several times attacked by pirates) once occupied by one of the most powerful families on the island, the owners of huge sugar-cane plantations. The house is now a tomato-packing station.

Situation and characteristics

The town

*Barranco del Infierno

The Barranco del Infierno (Gorge of Hell) is a huge canyon-like gorge immediately north-east of Adeje. It is reached by turning off the main street at the Church of St Úrsula into the road to the Casa Fuerte and, before reaching the house, taking a paved road on the right which ends at the entrance to the Barranco del Infierno.

The narrow path through the Barranco leads into one of the most beautiful stretches of scenery on Tenerife. At first we encounter only the sparse vegetation characteristic of the southern part of the island, but the farther we advance into the gorge the more luxuriant does the plant life become. The Barranco owes its rich growth of vegetation to the stream which flows through it; but since the water of the stream is carried down into the valley in canals, it is not encountered until lower down the gorge. The path, which is well made but becomes impassable after heavy rain, then crosses the stream several times. At the end of the gorge a waterfall plunges down

◄ Mount Teide, Tenerife

Barranco de Infierno   *Waterfall*

from cliffs over 1000 m (3300 ft) high in a distance of some 80 m (260 ft), forming at the foot a tiny lake of crystal-clear water. The waterfall is not particularly impressive in itself, but it is an unusual phenomenon in the Canaries, which are poorly supplied with springs and perennial watercourses.

In spite of notices which say otherwise, this is an easy walk taking little more than 2 or 3 hours there and back. Stout footwear is advisable, but there is no need for great agility or a good head for heights.

Anaga Hills

See Las Montañas de Anaga

Arafo   C9

Altitude: 510 m (1675 ft)
Population (district): 3700

Situation and characteristics

Arafo lies 20 km (12½ miles) south-west of Santa Cruz, near the pilgrimage centre of Candelaria.

This little settlement is noted for its musical and cultural traditions, and the ceremonies at the end of August in honour of its patron saint attract large numbers of visitors.

The village

An attractive village of whitewashed houses, it is surrounded by fruit orchards and vineyards. The church (carved woodwork in the interior) is of only local importance.

Montaña de las Arenas

To the west of Arafo rises the Montaña de las Arenas, also known as the Volcán de Arafo. During a series of eruptions in 1705 and 1706 masses of lava flowed down from the volcano on the seaward side.

Arico   C/D9

Altitude: 575 m (1885 ft)
Population (district): 4300

Arico, a charming hill village incorporating a number of separate communes, lies some 45 km (28 miles) south-west of Santa Cruz. The inhabitants live by farming, growing mainly potatoes and tomatoes in the terraced fields surrounding the village.

Situation and characteristics

The village church, the Iglesia de San Juan Bautista, dates from the 17th c.

The village

Poris de Abona

On the coast some 6 km (4 miles) from Arico is the fishing village of Poris de Abona, with a holiday development of apartments and bungalows. There are facilities for bathing, but no sandy beaches: these are to be found at the Punta de Abona, 2 km (1¼ miles) south, and the Punta del Rincón, 2·5 km (1½ miles) north.

Arona   D7

Altitude: 632 m (2074 ft)
Population (district): 18,000

Arona, 10 km (6 miles) north of Los Cristianos, is the chief place in its district, which also includes the Costa del Silencio, Los Cristianos and part of Playa de las Américas (see entries).

Situation and characteristics

The houses of this little town are scattered over the hillside on both sides of the main road. In the centre of the town stands the parish church, with an aisleless nave.

The town

Roque del Conde

Above Arona rears the Roque del Conde (1003 m (3291 ft)), a flat-topped hill from which there are fascinating panoramic views. To climb the hill, leave Arona on the road to the village of Vento. From here a path leads up to the summit (9 km (5½ miles) there and back). The summit plateau was formerly used for the growing of grain; it is now carpeted with flowers in spring.

Bajamar   A9

Altitude: sea-level
Population: 2800

Situation and characteristics

Bajamar (Down by the Sea), at the foot of the Anaga Hills in north-eastern Tenerife, is one of the oldest tourist settlements on the island. This is a favourite place for a restful holiday or for a longer stay.

The resort

Numbers of hotels, apartment blocks and bungalows extend along the coast and the gentle slopes above it. Because of the heavy surf sea-bathing is not to be recommended, but there are seawater swimming-pools along the promenade, and the hotels also have pools. Along the main streets are numerous cafés, restaurants, shops and banks.

Punta del Hidalgo

3 km (2 miles) north-east of Bajamar on the coast road is Punta del Hidalgo, an old fishing village which has been transformed by the building of large hotel complexes but nevertheless, like Bajamar, provides facilities for a restful holiday. The rocky coast offers good fishing; for bathers and sunbathers there are seawater swimming-pools.

Barranco del Infierno

See Adeje

*Bosque de la Esperanza   B9

Situation

The Bosque de la Esperanza (Esperanza Forest) extends along the Cumbre Dorsal, the ridge of hills which runs north-east from the gigantic crater of Las Cañadas and falls down on the north to the plateau of La Laguna.

The Bosque de la Esperanza is best reached from La Laguna on the Carretera Dorsal (Ridgeway), which runs south-west from the town to Las Cañadas. The forest begins soon after the village of La Esperanza, at an altitude of about 700 m (2300 ft).

The forest

Huge Canary pines (*Pinus canariensis*) and eucalyptus trees grow in the Bosque de la Esperanza. The forest lies in the misty trade-wind zone which favours the dense growth of trees. Water condenses on the long needles of the pines and on the other plants, seeps into the volcanic rocks and accumulates in underground cavities floored with impermeable rock.

Viewpoints

Running up from La Laguna towards Las Cañadas, the

Carretera Dorsal offers a succession of magnificent views –
provided always that visibility is not obscured by the morning
mists. The finest viewpoints are the Mirador Pico de las Flores
(1310 m (4300 ft); view of La Laguna Plateau and Anaga
Hills), El Diabillo (1600 m (5250 ft); views on both sides of the
ridge) and the Mirador de Ortuño (1804 m (5920 ft); view of
La Victoria).

La Esperanza

The village of La Esperanza, 6 km (4 miles) south-west of La
Laguna, is noted for the manufacture of the *esperancera*, the
typical Canary blanket, still worn as a cloak by some peasants
and shepherds.

2 km (1¼ miles) south of La Esperanza a side road diverges from   Las Raíces
the Carretera Dorsal on the left to Las Raíces, where on 17 June
1936 General Franco assembled the garrison of the island of
Tenerife in order to plan his military coup on mainland Spain
(17–18 July 1936). There is a commemorative stone.

Bosque de las Mercedes

See Las Montañas de Anaga

Buenavista (Buenavista del Norte)   **B6**

Altitude: 122 m (400 ft)
Population (district): 4600

Buenavista lies at the foot of the Teno Hills in north-western   Situation and characteristics
Tenerife, some 35 km (22 miles) from Santa Cruz. It is the chief
place in the district of the same name.

There are a number of handsome 17th and 18th c. houses   The town
round the plaza. Also in the square stands the Church of the
Virgen de los Remedios, which contains an ornate retablo and
a painting of St Francis by Alonso Cano (1601–67).

Punta de Teno

From Buenavista a road leads west to the Punta de Teno, the
most westerly point on Tenerife. The asphalt surface comes
to an end a little way outside the town, but the rough track
which continues beyond this is perfectly practicable with care
and patience. The distance there and back is about 20 km
(12½ miles), and the trip takes between 40 and 60 minutes.
The road to the Punta de Teno passes a number of lonely farms.
In clear weather the island of La Palma can be seen.

6 km (4 miles) from Buenavista on the Punta de Teno road is a   *Mirador de Don Pompeyo
fine viewpoint, the Mirador de Don Pompeyo, with a mag-
nificent prospect of the rocky coast and the little town of
Buenavista, surrounded by banana plantations.

Faro de Teno

On the Punta de Teno stands a lighthouse, the Faro de Teno. Until a few years ago a lighthouse-keeper lived here, but the house beside the lighthouse is now abandoned. Nowadays the promontory is frequented only by a few fishermen trying their luck on the rocky coast and occasional holiday visitors in tents or caravans.

**Caldera de las Cañadas   C7/8

Situation

The Caldera de las Cañadas, together with Mount Teide (see Teide), forms the Parque Nacional del Teide (see entry), in the centre of Tenerife.

The Caldera

The Caldera de las Cañadas is a gigantic volcanic crater with a diameter of 16 km (10 miles) and a circumference of some 45 km (28 miles). It is bounded on the north by Mount Teide and on the east, south and west by high rock walls rising 500 m (1650 ft) above the plain. Within the crater are great expanses of scoria (*malpaíses*), and other masses of scoria rear up over smaller volcanoes and overlie earlier lava flows. The rocks show a wide range of colouring, from almost black to shades of red. The varied hues result from the oxidization of manganese in the rock; the most recent beds of lava with a manganese content are black. There are also extensive areas of obsidian, a brilliantly black rock, and areas in which light-coloured pumice predominates.
The bizarre rock formations to be found within the crater give this grandiose landscape an almost unreal character.

Origins

The term *caldera*, which comes from the island of La Palma (see entry), is applied to a volcanic crater of unusual width due to the effects of collapse and erosion. It is supposed that where Mount Teide now stands there was once a much larger volcanic peak, of which there remain only the high rock walls surrounding the Caldera de las Cañadas. The huge caldera came into existence when the centre of this earlier volcano collapsed after the ejection of a molten lava flow or as the result of an earthquake. The time when this occurred cannot be exactly established, but it is probable that the caldera was formed in the Late Tertiary era, perhaps 3 million years ago. The pressure exerted by the collapsed masses of rock forced the remaining magma upward, creating fresh cones of lava on the bottom of the caldera. This is thought to have been the origin of Mount Teide and probably also the earlier Pico Viejo.

Sights

Los Roques

Near the Parador Nacional is one of the most impressive rock formations in the Caldera de las Cañadas, known as Los Roques. These rocks, like the rock walls round the caldera, are probably a remnant of the earlier giant volcano.

Llano de Ucanca

From Los Roques there is a view to the west of the Llano de Ucanca, a wide plain. A small lake is usually formed here by snow-melt at the end of winter.

Los Roques, in the Caldera de las Cañadas ▶

Los Azulejos

The rocks known as Los Azulejos, a few hundred metres south-west of Los Roques, have long attracted the interest of the local people by their greenish colouring – the result of iron hydrates in the rock.

Paisaje Lunar

To the south of the Parador Nacional, near the Campamento Madre del Agua (holiday camp), can be seen the Paisaje Lunar (Lunar Landscape), a series of bizarrely shaped tufa columns unique in the Canaries. They can be reached by a short walk (7 km (4½ miles) there and back) from the Campamento Madre del Agua. The camp is approached by a road from Vilaflor and a track which branches off 4 km (2½ miles) above the village.

Candelaria   B9

Altitude: sea-level
Population (district): 7400

Situation and characteristics

On the coast 20 km (12½ miles) south-west of Santa Cruz, just off the Autopista del Sur, is the little town of Candelaria, the most important pilgrimage centre in the Canaries. Every year on 14–15 August thousands of islanders come here to do honour to the Virgen de la Candelaria, patroness of the archipelago.

The town

This little fishing town is dominated by its pilgrimage church, situated directly on the sea, on one side of a large plaza.
For holiday-makers there is a small beach of dark-coloured sand and also a seawater swimming-pool.

Llano de Ucana

Sights

The main feature of interest in Candelaria is the Basilica de
Nuestra Señora de la Candelaria. This new church, completed
in 1958, houses the most venerated object in the Canaries, the
image of the Virgen de la Candelaria.

The story goes that at the end of the 14th c., before the coming
of the Spaniards, the local Guanches found a figure of the
Virgin which had been washed up by the sea to the south of
present-day Candelaria. When they tried to throw stones at the
image their arms were paralysed. Thereafter the figure was
credited with miraculous powers and accorded great venera-
tion. During a storm and high tide in 1826 the image was
washed into the sea again; the present image was carved by
Fernando Estévez in 1830. The story of the Virgen de la
Candelaria is commemorated by a marble monument near the
church.

* Basilica de Nuestra Señora
de la Candelaria

Opening times:
Mon.–Fri. 7.30 a.m.–1 p.m.
and 3–8 p.m.; Sat., Sun, and
pub. hol. 7.30 a.m.–8 p.m.

On the seaward side of the square in which the church stands
are a number of massive sculptures of red volcanic stone. They
are said to represent the Guanche kings who ruled Tenerife
before the Spanish conquest.

Guanche statues

The parish church, the Iglesia de Santa Ana, dates from the
18th c. It contains a fine 17th c. Crucifix.

Iglesia de Santa Ana

Las Caletillas and Las Arenitas

3 km (2 miles) north of Candelaria are the two holiday

Basilica, Candelaria

developments of Las Caletillas and Las Arenitas with their tall hotel blocks. There are two bays with bathing beaches of dark-coloured sand, and Las Arenitas has seawater and freshwater swimming-pools.

Costa del Silencio   D/E8

Situation

The Costa del Silencio extends along the southernmost tip of Tenerife, a few kilometres west of the Reina Sofia Airport.
There are no sandy beaches on this stretch of coast, and bathing is possible only in a number of rocky coves, some of them with steps running down into the sea.

There are a number of holiday developments along the Costa del Silencio, centred on the hotel village of Ten Bel ("Ten" for Tenerife, "Bel" for Belgian), with apartment blocks and bungalows scattered about in the hilly countryside amid lush vegetation. Like other holiday villages in the area, Ten Bel has extensive facilities for sport and recreation. The numerous seawater swimming-pools make up for the lack of a bathing beach.

El Hierro

See Hierro

El Médano   D8

Altitude: sea-level
Population: 1300

Situation and characteristics

El Médano lies at the foot of the Montaña Roja (Red Hill, 171 m (561 ft)), close to the Reina Sofia Airport. It takes its name (*médano* = dune) from its sandy beach, the longest and finest on the island, extending for almost 2 km (1¼ miles) to the south-west of the resort.

El Médano will appeal not only to bathers and sunbathers but also to amateur botanists, with the flora of Saharan type which flourishes in the surrounding area. Here are found in relative abundance drought-loving species such as *Launaea arborescens, Zygophyllum fontanesii, Euphorbia balsamifera* and *Tamarix canariensis.*

The resort

El Médano, until recently a small fishing village, is now a developing tourist resort. It has already acquired two hotels of some size and numbers of small apartment blocks, built directly on the beach; but apart from these it is still a quiet little place, with a few cafés along the paved promenade and usually with only a few fishing-boats drawn up on the beach. With new hotels being built, change is in the air, but this is likely to remain a resort of modest size, in view of the strong winds which often blow here, carrying drifting sand with them. Although this may deter the sun-lovers, El Médano is attracting increasing

El Médano beach

numbers of wind-surfers (surfing school and hire of surf-boards on beach).

El Abrigo

From El Médano the coast road continues west to the fishing village of El Abrigo, which is noted for its many excellent fish restaurants.

3 km (2 miles) north-west of El Abrigo is a new golfing centre, Golf del Sur (see Practical Information – Sport). It is unexpected to find such an expanse of fresh green turf in the midst of this arid and barren landscape. Associated with the golf-course is a comfortable holiday settlement in traditional village style.

Golf del Sur

Fasnia   C9

Altitude: 400 m (1300 ft)
Population (district): 2300

Fasnia, chief place in the district of the same name, lies near the east coast of Tenerife some 40 km (25 miles) from Santa Cruz. It can be quickly reached on the Autopista del Sur. The settlement was founded in the 17th c.

Situation and characteristics

The principal landmark of Fasnia is the Montaña de Fasnia (406 m (1332 ft)), immediately adjoining the village. On the

The village

63

summit of the hill, from which there are extensive views of the coastal strip, is the Chapel of Nuestra Señora de los Dolores.

Volcán de Fasnia

North-west of Fasnia is a considerably larger hill, the Volcán de Fasnia (2176 m (7139 ft)). The last eruption was in 1705, when a lava flow stopped only just short of the village.
The ascent of the hill should be attempted only by experienced climbers.

Garachico   B7

Altitude: 10 m (33 ft)
Population (district): 4700

Situation
Garachico lies on the coast 25 km (15 miles) west of Puerto de la Cruz. Offshore is the striking Roque de Garachico.

History
Garachico was founded after the Spanish conquest of the island and, thanks to its harbour, from which much of Tenerife's wine was exported, rapidly developed into a thriving commercial town. Its prosperity was brought to an abrupt end by the eruption of the Volcán de Negro in 1706, when flows of lava filled in the harbour and covered almost the whole of the town. Garachico was rebuilt on the peninsula formed by the masses of lava, but it never recovered its earlier importance.

* The town
Garachico is an attractive little town with a pleasant shady plaza. In the square is a handsome Baroque palace, one of the few buildings surviving from the period before the eruption.

Sights

* Castillo de San Miguel
Overlooking the sea, near the harbour, stands the Castillo de San Miguel, which survived the 1706 eruption unscathed. Dating from the 16th c., it once belonged to the Counts of Gomera. Above the massive entrance doorway can be seen coats of arms and inscriptions.

Iglesia de Santa Ana
The Church of Santa Ana was built in the 18th c. on the foundations of earlier churches. It contains a figure of St Joachim by Luján Pérez.

Convento de San Francisco
The Convento de San Francisco, now the Casa de Cultura, also survived the volcanic eruption. Since this old Franciscan friary is used for various public events visitors sometimes have opportunities of seeing the interior and the beautiful cloister.

Gomera (La Gomera)   A/B3–5

Area: 378 sq. km (146 sq. miles)
Population: 20,000
Chief place: San Sebastián de la Gomera

Castillo de San Miguel

Doorway, San Miguel

Iglesia de Santa Ana

Gomera

Gomera, the second smallest of the Canary Islands (after Hierro), lies some 32 km (20 miles) west of Tenerife between latitude 28°14' and 28°1' N and between longitude 17°22' and 17°1' W.

The island's greatest length from north to south is 23 km (14 miles) and from east to west 25 km (15½ miles). These figures, however, give a misleading impression of the distances to be covered. Since the interior of the island is broken up by deep gorges (*barrancos*) the road from north to south follows a slow and winding course. Many of the imposing gorges open out in their lower reaches into wide valleys. Scattered about in these valleys and in the hills, which rise to 1487 m (4879 ft) in Mount Garajonay, are numbers of little villages and hamlets. To many visitors approaching Gomera on the ferry from Los Cristianos on Tenerife it seems a bare and rocky wilderness – an impression created by the sheer cliffs, up to 900 m (2950 ft) high, which ring the island, with only a few coves and beaches to provide relief. The realization that the interior of the island is covered with a lush growth of vegetation comes later.

Although Gomera is built up from volcanic rocks, like the other western Canaries, it differs from them in showing little in the way of volcanic landscape forms. This indicates that the last volcanic activity on the island occurred a very long time ago, probably as much as a million years ago.

Gomera comes second to La Palma in the abundance of its water-supply, with numerous springs and perennial water-courses in the interior and on the north and west coasts.

Like the other western Canaries, Gomera lies under the influence of the moist trade winds. Most of the rain falls in the north and west of the island; the east is drier, and it seldom rains in the south. In the centre of the island the annual rainfall is some 600 mm (24 in).

The relatively high rainfall and the island's natural water-supplies foster a lush growth of vegetation in the interior. Nowhere else in the Canaries are there so many palm groves as on Gomera. The Canary palm (*Phoenix canariensis*) grows wild mainly in the lower regions in the north and west. The interior of the island is covered with dense woodland. Here, in the Bosque del Cedro, are tree heaths and laurels which sometimes grow to a height of 20 m (65 ft). The lichens, up to 1 m (3 ft) long, which hang from the trees, give the area something of the air of a primaeval forest. The cedars from which the Bosque del Cedro takes its name no longer grow here. In the highest regions, pines flourish round Mount Garajonay, but while northern and central Gomera have a lush growth of vegetation the lower regions in the south and east have only a sparse plant cover. In these areas only drought-loving plants such as the spurges can flourish.

Gomera has suffered a sharp decline in population in recent years. It now has less than 20,000 inhabitants, compared with almost 30,000 in 1940. Evidence of this alarming decline is given by the almost depopulated settlements, particularly in the west and south of the island, and the villages in which families without men predominate. The explanation for the decrease in population lies in the poor economic prospects which have led

Luxuriant vegetation in the interior of Gomera ▶

many people to migrate to the larger Canary islands or to South America.

Economy

The island's principal source of income is still, as in the past, agriculture. The fertile volcanic soil and the rainfall in the north of the island provide favourable conditions for the growing of subtropical and tropical fruits. Although the fruit and vegetables mainly required for local consumption are grown by dry-farming methods, the bananas and tomatoes grown for export require irrigation. In the arid south, however, the wells required to provide an adequate water-supply can be afforded only by large farming units. Many places, particularly in the north of the island, are almost wholly dependent on the growing of bananas, and this can have disastrous economic consequences. The small Canary bananas are already almost unsaleable in world markets, and crops can be disposed of only with the aid of Government subsidies. In recent years increased efforts have been made to achieve some diversification, and avocados, mangoes and pawpaws are now being grown for export, though still on a modest scale.

Another important contribution to the island's economy is made by fishing. The catches – mainly cod and tunny – are sufficient to supply two fish-processing plants.

In recent years, too, the tourist and holiday trade has begun to play a part. Since the establishment of a regular ferry connection with Tenerife there has been a modest development of individual tourism, particularly in the Valle Gran Rey. Gomera has long been a favourite haunt of adherents of the "alternative society". In addition many holiday-makers on Tenerife make a day trip to Gomera. And if the plans for the

The barren landscape of eastern Gomera

construction of an airport on the island come to fruition within the near future this should give a further boost to tourism.

Exact knowledge of the history of Gomera dates only from the beginning of the 15th c., when the Norman adventurer Jean de Béthencourt, sailing in the Spanish service, landed on the island (1404). He established a small settlement but was unable to occupy the whole island. The Spaniard Fernando Ormel de Castro came to Gomera in 1438 but – for reasons that are still not understood – withdrew without achieving anything. In the mid 15th c., however, Hernán Peraza the Elder succeeded in conquering the island and establishing his authority, and in 1472 Gomera was officially made subject to the Spanish Crown and given the status of a *señorio*, a feudal possession. In 1487 the native population rose against Spanish rule, murdering Hernán Peraza the Younger; but Spanish authority was soon restored. Thereafter a relationship of peaceful coexistence between Spaniards and natives was established, and the two races gradually merged. The island remained a *señorio* until 1812.

History

An unusual form of communication has been preserved on Gomera – the "whistling language" (*silbo*), which may also have been practised on Tenerife at one time. This is not merely a code of sounds denoting particular events but a regular language in which the letters of the alphabet and certain syllables are represented by notes of different heights and strengths. This form of communication, which calls for long practice and precise differentiation of sounds on the part of both the "sender" and the "receiver", no doubt remained in use on Gomera because it suited the circumstances of rural life. With the whistling language it was possible to communicate across even the deepest gorges over a distance of 3–6 km (2–4 miles), depending on wind conditions. The receiver of a message could then pass it on, so that information could travel from end to end of the island within a very short time. Nowadays the people of Gomera tend to use the telephone more than the whistling language, which is difficult to learn. In order to preserve this means of communication, however, UNESCO has classed it as part of the world cultural heritage which should be protected.

El silbo

San Sebastián de la Gomera

The island's chief town and port, San Sebastián de la Gomera (San Sebastián for short), lies on the east coast at the mouth of the Barranco de la Villa. The town's modest little white houses fill the sheltered bay and climb up the steep and barren hillsides above it. The population of the town, including the adjoining communes, is just under 7000. It is a quiet little place, with the atmosphere of a village rather than a town; but twice daily, when the ferry comes in from Los Cristianos (Tenerife), it livens up. Since the planned airport has not yet been built the harbour provides its only contact with the outside world. San Sebastián has featured only briefly in history, when Columbus put in here on his voyages of discovery to take on provisions and water. Gomera likes to recall this glorious chapter in its past, which earned it the style of the "Isla Colombina".
Many visitors to Gomera pass quickly through the island's

General

capital – partly because of the modest appearance of the little town but also because the bathing beach beside the harbour does not appear particularly inviting.

Plaza Calvo Sotelo

The hub of the town's life, a few hundred metres from the harbour, is the Plaza Calvo Sotelo, shaded by tall laurel trees. The few features of interest in the town can be seen in a short walk, starting from here.

Ayuntamiento

In the square stands the Town Hall (Ayuntamiento) with its clock-tower, a modern building in traditional Canarian style.

Pozo de Colón

A few paces away, in the patio of the old Custom House, is the Pozo de Colón (Columbus's Well), from which Columbus is said to have drawn the water he required to suppy his ships. There is a commemorative tablet with the Spanish inscription, "With this water America was baptized".

Iglesia de la Asunción

From here we go along Calle del Medio, on the right-hand side of which is the Iglesia de la Asunción (Church of the Assumption), to which Columbus is said to have come for a final prayer before launching into the unknown. The foundation-stone of the church was laid in the 15th c.; the aisles and the arcades flanking the nave were added in the 16th c. The furnishings of the church are urgently in need of restoration: the wall-paintings are flaking off the walls, and the beautiful 15th c. wooden altar is in a state of dilapidation. A notable feature of the interior is the Puerta del Perdón (not preserved in its original condition). This Doorway of Pardon proved to be ill named. After the repression of the rising in

San Sebastián de la Gomera

First impressions of Gomera   *Torre del Conde*

which the Governor of the island, Hernán Peraza, was killed his widow Beatriz de Bobadilla held a service of reconciliation, promising that all who passed through the Puerta del Perdón and thus confessed their guilt would be pardoned but the promise was not kept and the rebels were executed.

Farther up Calle del Medio we come to another building associated with Columbus, the Casa Colombina. Every year about 6 September various cultural events and exhibitions are held here the Fiestas Colombinas, commemorating Columbus's connection with the town.

Casa Colombina

The most important historical monument in San Sebastián is the Torre del Conde, near the harbour. This Tower of the Count, in Castilian style, was built by Hernán Peraza the Elder in 1447 as part of the town's defences. Soon afterwards it provided a safe refuge for Beatriz de Bobadilla after the murder of her husband. In the 16th and 17th c. the 16 m (50 ft) high tower, the walls of which were strengthened in 1587, served for the safe keeping of booty brought back from America by the Conquistadors. This, of course, made the tower a favourite target for pirates, but it was never taken.
The tower now houses a small collection of liturgical utensils and art from South America. The museum has been closed for some years, but it is planned to extend the collection and open it to the public again.

Torre del Conde

From the harbour a tunnel passes through the steep rock face flanking the gorge to the Playa de la Cueva. On the stony and inhospitable beach is the Club Náutico.

Club Náutico

71

Palms in central Gomera

Playa de Hermigua

Parador Nacional
Conde de la Gomera

High above the town stands the Parador Nacional Conde de la Gomera, surely the finest hotel in the whole of the Canary Islands. It is reached by a narrow street which branches off Calle del Medio just beyond the Iglesia de la Asunción. Although it was built only in 1973 and enlarged in 1985 this has all the atmosphere of an old Canarian country house and the impression is reinforced by the historical paintings in some of the rooms.

Other places of interest on Gomera

The various places of interest on the island are described below in the form of a circular tour starting from San Sebastián. Although the distances involved are not great it takes quite a long time to get from place to place on the island's winding roads: at least two days should, therefore, be allowed for the tour.

Visitors on a day trip to Gomera from Los Cristianos (Tenerife) should limit themselves to part of the route. A good plan, for example, would be to take the road from San Sebastián via Hermigua to Agulo, return to Hermigua on the same road and then, 7 km (4½ miles) beyond this, take a narrow side road which penetrates the interior of the island and then curves round to return to San Sebastián.

From San Sebastián the Carretera del Norte runs north-west through a barren landscape; then, beyond the Tunel de la Cumbre, the scene changes and the road continues through luxuriant vegetation.

From the Mirador de la Carbonera, a short distance beyond the tunnel, there is a wide prospect of lush green interior of the island. The view takes in the Barranco de Monte Forte and, in the distance, the white houses of Hermigua.

Mirador de la Carbonera

Hermigua, the second largest place on the island, is surrounded by banana plantations. Its houses extend down the gorge to the Playa de Hermigua. There is a 16th c. monastic church containing a fine image of Nuestra Señora de la Encarnación by the 19th c. Spanish sculptor Fernando Estévez. In the Plaza de San Pedro can be found a small private ethnological museum. Also of interest is the craft exhibition of Los Telares, which has a number of rooms containing spinning and domestic equipment of earlier times but is mainly devoted to the display and sale of fabrics woven on old looms and beautiful local pottery.

*Hermigua

3 km (2 miles) north-east of Hermigua, at the foot of formidable rock walls, lies Agulo, which is worth visiting if only for the sake of the fine view of the town on its low hill which can be had from the main road, against the majestic backdrop of Mount Teide, almost always capped by a ring of clouds.

*Agulo

The road now continues on its winding course, passes the beautifully situated Las Rosas restaurant and comes to Vallehermoso with its striking landmark, the Roque Cano (Dog Rock), the vent of an old volcano which has been laid bare by erosion.
From Vallehermoso a short detour (4 km (2½ miles)) can be made to Puerto Vallehermoso. Only remnants of the harbour

Vallehermoso

Agulo, with Mount Teide in the background

installations survive; after the harbour ceased to be used they were left to rot. The heavy surf sometimes makes bathing hazardous here.

*Los Órganos

From Puerto Vallehermoso, therefore, there are boat trips to Los Órganos, a few kilometres north-west in the Bay of La Playita, only in good weather. This imposing stretch of cliffs, 200 m (220 yd) long and over 80 m (260 ft) high, made up of large numbers of basalt columns resembling organ pipes, regularly arranged on different levels, can be seen only from the sea.

There are also boat trips from Valle Gran Rey and San Sebastián.

**Valle Gran Rey

The road winds down through the village of Arure, which was probably one of the main settlements on the island in pre-Hispanic times, into the Valle Gran Rey (Valley of the Great King), with the village of that name. This long valley with its terraced fields, its profusion of palms, its large banana plantations and its scatter of little houses has a strikingly exotic aspect. In recent years many "drop-outs", drawn by the charm of the valley, have made their home here, and the fertile valley with the beaches at its mouth has become a stronghold of the "alternative" culture. At the mouth of the valley, on the island's most westerly point, are the villages of Calera, La Playa Calera and Vueltas, each with its own distinctive atmosphere. Calera, perched on the hillside amid banana plantations, is one of the most beautiful villages in the Canaries; La Playa Calera is a beach settlement; Vueltas is a fishing village centred on its harbour.

Vallehermoso

To continue the circuit of the island it is necessary to return to Arure, where a road goes off to Las Hayas and El Cercado. El Cercado has a number of workshops producing native pottery made without the use of a wheel. This pottery is often called Chipude ware, from a collective name which was formerly applied to a number of local hamlets (Temocodá, Pavón, etc.), but this name no longer appears on any signpost.

El Cercado

For a beautiful view of the hills in the centre of Gomera, take the road which returns (north) to Las Hayas. 2 km (1¼ miles) beyond this village a road branches off on the right to the viewpoint of La Laguna Grande. Set in a clearing (restaurant), this is a favourite starting-point for walks and climbs in the central massif. From here there is a road to the Ermita de Nuestra Señora de Lourdes. Here the Fiesta del Cedro is celebrated annually on the last Sunday in August with a procession to the tiny village of El Cedro and various popular festivities. Farther along the road is the village of Igualero, from which a forest track climbs up to Mount Garajonay, the island's highest peak (1487 m (4879 ft)). From the summit there are superb views of Gomera and the neighbouring islands.

**Parque Nacional de Garajonay (Bosque del Cedro)

From Igualero it is 20 km (12½ miles) to San Sebastián by way of the excellent road which crosses the island from west to east.

Alternatively it is possible to continue south from Igualero to Playa de Santiago, the sunniest place on the island, where a modest tourist trade is gradually developing. The little town is still, however, mainly dependent on fishing; its economy was given a boost when the Norwegian-owned Olsen Line, which operates the ferry between Los Cristianos and San Sebastián, established a fish-processing plant here.
The return to San Sebastián is on the Carretera del Sur.

Playa de Santiago

Shortly before the road reaches San Sebastián the Monumento al Sagrado Corazón de Jesús (Monument to the Sacred Heart of Jesus) can be seen on a hill to the right. This is a 7 m (23 ft) high figure of Christ on a 10 m (33 ft) high base, erected in 1958. From here there are good views of San Sebastián and the island of Tenerife.

Monumento al Sagrado Corazón de Jesús

Granadilla de Abona   D8

Altitude: 654 m (2146 ft)
Population (district): 14,000

The little town of Granadilla de Abona lies in a fertile region in the south of Tenerife, some 10 km (6 miles) north of the Reina Sofia Airport. It is an important road junction, situated at the intersection of the main north–south road with a road running from east to west, and one of the island's largest agricultural centres. Vegetables, potatoes, corn and vines are grown in the area.

Situation and characteristics

Although it is the chief place in southern Tenerife Granadilla has little to offer the visitor. It is a modest little town, with its unpretentious houses lining the main road but it has no buildings of particular interest.

The town

Guía de Isora   C7

Altitude: 612 m (2008 ft)
Population (district): 11,000

Situation and characteristics

The little town of Guía de Isora in western Tenerife, near the holiday settlement of Los Gigantes, owes its prosperity to the discovery of abundant supplies of water. Situated outside the area of influence of the moist trade winds, it was previously restricted to a very modest development of agriculture; but with the help of irrigation from its circular storage tanks it now produces good crops, mainly of tomatoes and bananas.

The town

The most important building in this trim little town is the Iglesia de la Virgen de la Luz, which stands in the plaza. This Renaissance church with Mudéjar features was restored in its original style in the 1950s. It contains a number of works (including the figure of the Virgen de la Luz) by the Canarian sculptor Luján Pérez.

Güimar   C9

Altitude: 289 m (948 ft)
Population (district): 13,500

Situation and characteristics

Güimar, 25 km (15 miles) south-west of Santa Cruz, is the chief place in the Valle de Güimar. The surrounding area was apparently settled in pre-Hispanic times, for numerous Guanche burial-places and dwellings have been found in caves here.

The town

This neat and busy little town is laid out on a spacious scale. Above the main street rises the Iglesia de San Pedro Apóstol, which has a fine statue of St Peter.

Mirador de Don Martín

The best view of Güimar and its valley is to be had from the Mirador de Don Martín, above the town to the south-west. In the background can be seen Santa Cruz and the Anaga Hills.

Volcán de Güimar

There are also wide-ranging views from the summit of the Volcán de Güimar (276 m (906 ft)) to the east of the town, near the Autopista del Sur. The crater of the volcano is 300 m (330 yd) in circumference and 60 m (200 ft) deep.

Puerto de Güimar

4 km (2½ miles) east of Güimar lies the fishing village of Puerto de Güimar. Although the coast in this area is not particularly inviting, a number of apartment blocks and hotels have been built here.

Hierro (El Hierro)   C–E3–5

Area: 277 sq. km (107 sq. miles)
Population: 6000
Chief place: Valverde

Hierro, the most westerly of the Canaries, lies 128 km (80 miles) from Tenerife between latitude 27°53' and 27°37' N and between longitude 18°14' and 17°49' W.

Hierro is the smallest of the seven main Canary islands, measuring only 24 km (15 miles) from north to south and 27 km (17 miles) from west to east. The island is of volcanic origin: the semicircular bay on the north side, El Golfo, is probably the remnant of a mighty northern crater rim whose northern half has been engulfed by the sea. Numerous younger volcanoes have broken through the older volcanic deposits. Although there have been no eruptions within historical times the evidence of volcanic activity is still clearly visible: most of the coasts, for example, are fringed by massive lava flows which look quite fresh.

Topography

At first sight the island, surrounded by cliffs up to 1000 m (3300 ft) high and with only a few small stretches of beach, looks distinctly inhospitable. Inland is an upland region rising to 1500 m (4900 ft) in Mount Malpaso. This area and the lower area on the north side of the island offer the most favourable conditions for settlement and agriculture.

Hierro has no springs (apart from the sulphurous spring of Sabinosa) or perennial watercourses, and since rainfall is low and such rain as falls seeps rapidly away in the permeable volcanic rock, water-supply has always been a problem on the island. This is shown by the numerous legends about the water-dispensing *árbol santo* (sacred tree), known to the original inhabitants as *garoé*. It is said that the water which condensed from the clouds and dripped from the long needles of the tree was sufficient to supply the needs of the whole population of Amoco (now Valverde). The tree was uprooted by a whirlwind in the early 17th c.

There are a variety of explanations for the name of the island. The Spanish name Hierro (originally Ferro) means "iron" but since there is no iron on the island this cannot be the original meaning. Some authorities suggest a derivation from *hero*, which meant "water-container" in the old language of the Canaries; others refer it to the term *esoro* used by the Greek geographer Ptolemy, meaning "strong" or "holy".

The island's name

Although the annual rainfall is only 300 m (12 in), the frequent mists at heights of over 500 m (1650 ft), particularly on the north-east side of the island, bring additional moisture. The central area and the west and south coasts have a more equable and sunnier climate.

Climate

In these climatic conditions land below 500 m (1650 ft) supports a vegetation of succulents. At higher levels, particularly round the Bay of El Golfo, there are remains of the original forest cover of laurels, cedars and pines. Above 1300 m (4265 ft) are the great expanses of pine forest which are the characteristic feature of Hierro.

Vegetation

Hierro has a population of some 6000 (Herreños). This figure was reached at the turn of the 19th c.; by the time of the Second World War it had risen to some 9000; but since then it has regularly declined or stagnated – a consequence of the limited

Population

opportunities for making a living on the island which have led many Herreños to emigrate (in the past mainly to South America, particularly Venezuela).

Economy

The island's main source of income is agriculture, though this is inevitably restricted by the shortage of water. The main crops are wine, tomatoes, potatoes, almonds, peaches, bananas and pineapples. Most of the farmers have smallholdings; only bananas and pineapples, largely destined for export, are grown on large plantations.

Stock-farming (mainly sheep and goats) is limited by the restricted areas of pasture. Fishing, practised off the south coast, makes only a modest contribution to the economy; the catches are not sufficient to justify the establishment of a fish-processing plant on the island.

The exports of agricultural produce leave Hierro with a large deficit on its balance of trade. Much of the island's everyday requirements must be imported, and imports are subsidized by exemption from Value Added Tax. The development of tourism has barely begun. In recent years the roads have been improved and the fine Parador Nacional of El Hierro has been built, but the number of individual tourists is still small. There are ambitious plans for the future, providing for a tenfold increase in the number of beds available (at present 300).

History

The history of the island before the Spanish conquest is obscure. All that is known for certain is that Arab seamen had found their way to Hierro before the coming of the Spaniards. Spanish influence first reached Hierro with Jean de Béthencourt's landing in 1405. Subsequently much of the male population was carried off to Europe as slaves, and Norman and Castilian peasants were settled on the island, gradually merging with the surviving indigenous inhabitants – a process which had been completed by the end of the 15th c. In 1515 Hierro became a *señorio*, with obligations to pay dues to the Counts of Gomera and the Spanish Crown. This feudal structure survived into the early 19th c.

Hierro featured in history at the time of Columbus's voyages of discovery, when it was the starting-point of his second expedition to America in 1493. Otherwise it remained remote from great events. In more recent times its remoteness gave it a new role under Franco's dictatorship, when it became a place of banishment for opponents of the régime.

It was only in the 1970s, following the great social and economic changes of recent years (electrification, development of water-supplies and irrigation, improvements in the educational system, etc.) and the construction of an airport, that the island awoke from its sleep and established new links with Europe.

In the 2nd c. A.D. the Greek scientist and geographer Ptolemy took the western cape of Hierro as the most westerly point in the world and designated it as the "end of the world". As a result the western tip of the island, the Punta de Orchilla, was

El Golfo ▶

Hierro: pinewoods...   *...and vineyards*

selected in 1634 as the prime meridian, to be generally superseded by Greenwich only in 1884.

Valverde

General

Valverde, the chief place on Hierro (pop. 2000), lies in the north-east of the island, 7 km (4½ miles) from the airport and 10 km (6¼ miles) from Hierro's principal port, Puerta Estaca. It still justifies its name (Valverde=Green Valley), being surrounded by fruit orchards, fields of vegetables and flower gardens. It can be cool and windy when the trade winds are blowing, but at other times is a friendly and inviting little place.

The indigenous inhabitants of the island had a settlement here, which they called Amoco; but Valverde became the administrative centre of Hierro only after the Spanish conquest. The present layout of the town dates from the end of the 15th c.

Sights

Below the town's two main streets stands the Iglesia de la Concepción (Church of the Conception), originally a fortified church designed to provide protection against pirate raids. The present three-aisled church was built in the late 18th c. on the remains of its predecessor of 1544.

Valverde has two small museums (irregular opening times). The Exposición de Fondos Etnográficos y Arqueológicos (Calle Licenciado Bueno 1) is a collection of old household equipments, cult objects, jewellery and much other material dating from the time of the Bimbaches, as the indigenous inhabitants of Hierro were known, and from the Spanish conquest.

Iglesia de la Concepción Valverde

The Museo Juan Padrón, a small private museum in a typical old Canarian house at Calle Previsor Magdalena 8, also has an interesting collection of material from both pre-Hispanic and Spanish times but it is worth seeing for the sake of its beautiful patio alone.

Other places of interest on Hierro

The other places of interest on Hierro are described below in the form of a round trip starting from Valverde. It should be remembered, however, that the roads in the west of the island are mainly forest tracks, not always easily practicable for cars, and that even a short drive may take a long time. It is preferable, therefore, to explore the western half of Hierro on foot.

Going north-west from Valverde, the road passes through the villages of Mocanal and Guarazoca and comes to the Mirador de la Peña (*c.* 10 km (6 miles)). Here there is a building of glass and reddish lava stone, designed by the well-known Lanzarote architect César Manrique (see Notable Personalities), which is destined to house a restaurant. Like the various outlook terraces which have been constructed here, it fits beautifully into the landscape.

Mirador de la Peña

From the mirador there is an extensive view over the bay of El Golfo, with its sheer rock faces ranging up to 1000 m (3300 ft), its fertile expanse of plain below the cliffs and its many villages and hamlets of whitewashed houses. At the east end of the bay, to the north of the viewpoint, are the Roques de Salmor, rising

**El Golfo

81

Mirador de la Peña: restaurant . . .   *. . . and view*

out of the sea to a height of almost 100 m (330 ft). Until recent years this was the habitat of a giant lizard, *Gallotia simonyi*, which reached a length of up to 1 m (40 inches). The last representatives of the species have now withdrawn to the almost inaccessible rocky terrain below the mirador.

Beyond the mirador the road continues to climb, passing through a fairly barren landscape and then entering the aromatic pine forests on the plateau.

San Andrés

The road soon comes to San Andrés, a good base for walks and climbs in the surrounding area.

Mirador de Jinama

A few kilometres along the road to Frontera a narrow side road goes off to the Mirador de Jinama, from which there is another fantastic view of El Golfo. Near the mirador is a small chapel, the Ermita de la Caridad.

Frontera

The road traverses dense pine forests and then winds its way down amid vineyards to Frontera. Situated in the most extensive fruit- and wine-growing region on Hierro, this is the second largest place on the island and the administrative centre of its southern and western part. The village church has a separate belfry, prominently situated on a volcanic cone.

*Sabinosa

12 km (7½ miles) from Frontera, in the north-west of Hierro, is Sabinosa. It owes its name to a species of juniper, *Juniperus sabina*, which formerly grew in abundance on the hills above the village. The remaining specimens of this coniferous species, which is peculiar to Hierro, are under statutory protection.

Sabinosa is noted for its sulphurous medicinal spring, the Pozo de la Salud, 3 km (2 miles) from the village. The present installations for "taking the cure" are very modest, but it is planned to build new and modern facilities.

If time permits, a detour can be made to the remote coastal area of Arena Blanca with its rare flora.

From the Pozo de la Salud there is a surfaced road to the Santuario de Nuestra Señora de los Reyes. In this small chapel in the Plain of La Dehesa (Pastureland) the image of the island's patroness is preserved. According to legend this statue of the Virgin was given to some local shepherds on 6 January 1546, in exchange for water and provisions, by seamen whose vessel had inexplicably stuck fast in a bay. The shepherds carried the image up from the bay on a donkey and saw to their astonishment that the ship had suddenly been released and continued its voyage. Subsequently the Virgin was said to have relieved the island on several occasions from severe droughts. Then in January 1714, after a long period of drought, the Virgin was carried from her chapel in the Plain of La Dehesa to Valverde in a plea for rain. When rain thereupon began to fall in abundance it was resolved to carry the Virgin in procession to Valverde every four years and to make her patroness of the island. (The next processions are due to be held in 1989, 1993, etc.) In order to make it easier for Herreños who had left the island to take part in the celebrations the date of the Bajada (Descent) of the Virgen de los Reyes was later moved to the first week-end in July.

The route of the procession from the little chapel can be followed either on foot or by car.

Frontera . . .

. . . and its belfry

83

Hierro

Cruz de los Humilladeros
Malpaso

The route leads past the Cruz de los Humilladeros to the island's highest peak, Mount Malpaso (1500 m (4922 ft)). From the top there are views of the island in all directions.

*Los Letreros

Continuing the tour of the island, from the Santuario de Nuestra Señora de los Reyes we take the forest track which runs east to the villages of Las Casas and Taibique. A path (not suitable for cars) diverges from this track to the rock-cut inscriptions of Los Letreros. Since these important inscriptions have suffered in recent years from the attentions of souvenir-hunters the island government has barred the road to them. To see the inscriptions, some of which are badly weathered, it is necessary to have written authority from the island authorities and a good local guide.

The inscriptions were discovered in 1870 by a priest, Don Aquilino Padrón, whose interest had been aroused by the place-name Los Letreros (The Inscriptions). The date and significance of the inscriptions have not been established; it is clear, however, that characters belonging to different periods are found on the same rock face. Two forms of pictographic script – a primitive type of script conveying merely concepts and ideas – have been distinguished, and there is also evidence of a more complex system of characters which shows analogies with our own alphabetic script. Another variant, using both types of character, reflects the transition from a purely pictographic to an alphabetic script.

The Los Letreros area must once have been an important cult site, as is shown by the finds of animal bones, the remains of a *tagoror* (a circular place of assembly hewn from stone) and the *conchero*, a layer of shells almost a metre thick.

Hoya del Morcillo

Continuing east on the forest track, we come, shortly before Las Casas, to the recreation area of Hoya del Morcillo (barbecue installations, wooden tables and benches, toilet facilities), a picnic place much favoured by the islanders, particularly at week-ends.

Las Casas/Taibique

The two villages of Las Casas and Taibique in the south-east of the island, now amalgamated under the name of El Pinar, have maintained old spinning and weaving traditions.

A few kilometres north of Las Casas a path branches off the main road to San Andrés and runs east to the Mirador de las Playas. The path itself, passing through beautiful pine woods, is rewarding enough, but even finer is the magnificent view over the wide Bay of Las Playas.

There is another mirador at the south end of Taibique, with a view which ranges from the terraced fruit and vegetable fields round the village to the rugged cliffs of the Punta de la Restinga.

La Restinga

10 km (6 miles) from Taibique, at the southern tip of Hierro, is La Restinga, one of the youngest settlements on the island. The inhabitants live mainly by fishing. To protect the harbour from the stormy sea a breakwater was built in 1978, and this also provides shelter for bathers.

To see some further features of interest on Hierro, it is necessary
to return to Valverde (32 km (20 miles) from La Restinga).

From Valverde a good road leads east to the Aeropuerto de
Hierro (8 km (5 miles)), which came into service in 1972. After
seeing the alarmingly short runway it will come as no surprise
to learn that in unfavourable wind conditions the Iberia flights
are sometimes unable to land.

Aeropuerto de Hierro

A short distance before the airport a side road branches off to
Tamaduste, the islanders' most popular place of recreation.
Flanking the sheltered bay (the most easily accessible bathing
beach on Hierro) numbers of trim little week-end houses have
been built in recent years.

Tamaduste

8 km (5 miles) south of Tamaduste is the island's port, Puerto
Estaca, which until the construction of the airport handled all
traffic to and from Hierro. It gets its name from the mooring-
pole (*estaca*) to which the fishermen tied their boats.
Until the beginning of the 20th c. passengers and goods had
to be brought to land in small boats. It was only after King
Alfonso XIII had suffered an involuntary ducking during
transhipment in 1906 that it was resolved to build a pier.

Puerto Estaca

Soon after Puerto Estaca on the road to Valverde a minor road
goes off to the Parador Nacional El Hierro, a handsome hotel in
traditional Castilian style built between 1973 and 1976. Owing
to difficulties encountered in building the access road,
however, the hotel could not be opened until 1981 (photo-
graph, p. 163).

Parador Nacional El Hierro

Puerto Estaca

Roques Bonanza

°Roques Bonanza

Shortly before reaching the parador the road passes a bizarre rock formation known as the Roques Bonanza, a mass of tufa and basalt eroded by the sea which lies only a few metres from the shore.

The return to Valverde is on the same road as on the outward journey (*c.* 15 km (9 miles)).

Icod de los Vinos B7

Altitude: 235 m (771 ft)
Population (district): 19,000

Situation and characteristics

Icod de los Vinos lies some 20 km (12¼ miles) west of Puerto de la Cruz in a fertile valley above the coast. As its name indicates, the town, which was founded in 1501, is famous for its wine. Most visitors come to Icod to see the oldest and finest dragon tree (*Dracaena draco*) in the Canaries.

°The town

The old part of the town, round the Iglesia de San Marcos, is trim and attractive. The gardens in the square in front of the church and round the dragon tree contribute to its charm. The little street which leads up between the square and the dragon tree leads to another beautiful square planted with palms (including a rarity, an eight-branched washingtonia) and other old trees.

A shady avenue goes past the church to the newer part of the town, which during business hours is a scene of hectic activity, with people and cars thronging the narrow streets.

Sights

The Drago Milenario (Thousand-Year-Old Dragon Tree) is on the west side of the town. It stands over 16 m (50 ft) high and has a girth of some 6 m (20 ft). Its age is estimated at between 2000 and 3000 years – though some botanists believe that it is no more than a few hundred years old. Since the dragon tree forms no annual rings its age can be estimated only by the number of forks in the branches; but the branches fork at very irregular intervals, so that any estimate of age can only be very approximate. (See Facts and Figures – Flora and Fauna.)

**Drago Milenario

The house next to the dragon tree has a fine example of a traditional Canarian balcony, with house leeks (*Sempervivum tectorum*) growing on its roof.

Above the gardens surrounding the dragon tree stands the Iglesia de San Marcos (15th–16th c.), with a handsome Renaissance doorway. The ceiling of the church, made from the heartwood of the Canary pine, dates from the end of the 15th c. Other features of interest are the Baroque altar with its ornament of beaten silver, the Rococo woodcarving in the Capilla de los Dolores and the figure of San Diego de Alcalá by the Spanish sculptor Pedro de Mena y Medrano (1628–88).

Iglesia de San Marcos

*San Marcos

The road running north from Icod ends in 3 km (2 miles) at the little fishing port of San Marcos, with a number of restaurants

The dragon tree of Icod

bordering the beach of black sand to tempt the visitor. It is a
picturesque scene – if one or two new tower blocks can be
ignored – with rugged cliffs fringing the little bay.

Cueva del Rey

In the rocky surrounding country a number of caves used by the
Guanches for burial have been discovered. 2 km (1¼ miles) east
of San Marcos is the Cueva del Rey (local guide essential).

La Gomera

See Gomera

La Laguna (San Cristóbal de la Laguna)   B10

Altitude: 550 m (1805 ft)
Population: 113,000

Situation and characteristics

La Laguna (officially San Cristóbal de la Laguna), the largest
and most important town on Tenerife after Santa Cruz, lies in
the fertile Aguere Plain in the north-east of the island. It owes
its importance mainly to the fact that it is the seat of the only
university in the Canaries and, as the see of a bishop, the
religious centre of the province of Santa Cruz de Tenerife.

History

The town was founded in 1496 by the conqueror of Tenerife,
Alonso Fernández de Lugo, who made it his residence and
the administrative capital of the whole archipelago. A factor
in the choice of the site may have been the small lake (now
dried up) from which the town takes its name. La Laguna
rapidly developed into the political and intellectual centre
of the Canaries, a status which it retained until superseded
bySanta Cruz in 1723. The first university was founded by
Augustinian Canons in 1701; the present Provincial University dates from 1817. La Laguna has been an episcopal see
since 1818.

**The town

La Laguna is often thought to be the most Spanish town in the
Canaries. It has preserved its original chequer-board plan and
numerous handsome burghers' houses and noble mansions,
impressive examples of the Spanish Colonial style of the 16th
and 17th c. These features are of course found only in the old
central area of the town. Since the middle of the 20th c. La
Laguna has experienced a substantial growth in population,
and its modern suburbs continue to expand. Nevertheless La
Laguna has much more of a "small-town" atmosphere than
one would expect in a university city of over 100,000
inhabitants.

Viewpoints

There are superb views of La Laguna and the intensively
cultivated surrounding valley from the Cruz del Carmen and
the Mirador Pico del Inglés on the fringes of the Anaga Hills
and from the Mirador Pico de las Flores and many other
viewpoints on the road which ascends from La Laguna to Las
Cañadas.

Sights

A good starting-point for a tour of La Laguna is the shady Plaza del Adelantado, round which are a number of handsome houses with carved wooden balconies and doorways bearing coats of arms. In the centre of the square can be seen a fountain of white marble decorated with lions' heads.

At the north-east corner of the square stands the Palacio de Nava, a typical example of Spanish Colonial Baroque. Adjoining it is the Convent of Santa Catalina.

Plaza del Adelantado

The Neo-classical Town Hall (Ayuntamiento), at the corner of the square and Calle Obispo Rey Redondo, dates from the 19th c.; it contains wall-paintings illustrating the history of the island. Also in Calle Obispo Rey Redondo are the Casa de los Capitanes (17th c.), adjoining the Ayuntamiento, and the Theatre (No. 54).

Ayuntamiento

Farther along Calle Obispo Rey Redondo, in Plaza Fray Albino, we come to the Cathedral (Santa Iglesia Catedral). Originally founded in 1515, the Cathedral was given its present form at the beginning of this century, when, after several previous alterations, it was completely rebuilt. The white rendering of the Neo-classical façade was replaced at the beginning of the 1980s by a pink wash.

Although the exterior is relatively plain there are some major treasures of art in the interior. Among them are the metal screen between the choir and the Capilla Mayor, the tabernacle (by

*Cathedral

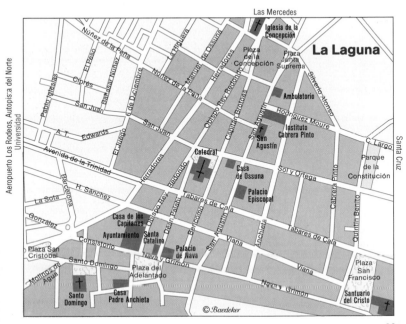

89

Luján Pérez), the marble pulpit (1767), the Baroque retablo in the Chapel of the Virgen de los Remedios and altar-pieces by the Flemish painter Hendrik van Balen (1575–1632), Van Dyck's master.

Behind the High Altar is the simple tomb of Alonso Fernández de Lugo (1456–1525), who initiated the building of the Cathedral.

Casa de Ossuna

A little way east of the Cathedral stands the Casa de Ossuna, with a private art collection.

*Iglesia de Nuestra Señora de la Concepción

Calle Obispo Rey Redondo continues to the Iglesia de Nuestra Señora de la Concepción, the oldest church in the town (built 1502). The tower, with Mudéjar features, was added about 1700. Having survived the centuries largely unchanged, the church now ranks as a national cultural monument.

The church's timber ceiling, a feature characteristic of the Canaries, dates from the 16th c. Finely carved, too, are the cedarwood pulpit, one of the finest in Spain, and the dark-coloured choir-stalls. At the other end of the church is the High Altar, of beaten silver. The 15th c. font of glazed tiles was used in the baptism of Guanche chieftains. Other features of interest are Luján Pérez's Mater Dolorosa and the figure of Nuestra Señora de la Concepción by Fernando Estévez.

Instituto Cabrera Pinto

The return to the starting-point of the tour can be by way of Calle de San Agustín. A few hundred metres along this street, on the left, is the Instituto Cabrera Pinto, a handsome building with a fine bell-tower.

Convento de San Agustín

A few paces farther down the street is a former Augustinian house (now rather dilapidated), the Convento de San Agustín, with the Iglesia de San Agustín.

Palacio Episcopal

Still farther south stands the 17th c. Palacio Episcopal (Bishop's Palace), with a fine Baroque façade.

Universidad de San Fernando

On the opposite side of the street can be seen the Old University (18th c.).

From here it is only a short distance to the Plaza del Adelantado. Alternatively, a detour can be made to the Santuario del Cristo, on the east side of the old town centre.

Santuario del Cristo

The Santuario del Cristo, a pilgrimage church in a Franciscan friary, possesses the most venerated figure of Christ in the Canaries, carved by a 15th c. Seville sculptor and brought to Tenerife by Alonso Fernández de Lugo in 1520.

If time permits it is worth taking a stroll through the modern part of La Laguna, on the west side of the town, with the New University.

Iglesia de Santo Domingo

On the way there we pass the Iglesia de Santo Domingo, in Calle Santo Domingo. Originally belonging to a Dominican monastery, it was built in the 16th and 17th c. in Plateresque style. It contains modern frescoes by Mariano de Cossio

Cathedral

Instituto Cabrera Pinto

(1890–1960), which are in sharp contrast to older works of art. In a garden adjoining the old conventual buildings can be seen a dragon tree which originally could vie in beauty with the one at Icod; although partly destroyed by lightning, it is still impressive.

Near the Autopista del Norte, set in gardens, is the New University, which dates from the mid 1950s.

University

Near by, in the large motorway roundabout, stands a monument commemorating José de Anchieta, a native of La Laguna who became the first Christian missionary in Brazil.

Monumento José de Anchieta

La Orotava

B8

Altitude: 345 m (1132 ft)
Population (district): 32,000

La Orotava lies above Puerto de la Cruz in the centre of the beautiful Orotava Valley (see Valle de la Orotava). One of the most attractive and most typical towns in the Canaries, it enjoys a climatically favoured situation which makes possible a highly productive agriculture.

Situation and characteristics

La Orotava was founded at the beginning of the 16th c. and rapidly grew into a thriving little settlement. In 1648 it was granted the status of town by a decree of Philip IV. Some years earlier it had acquired a port, Puerto de la Orotava (now Puerto

History

91

La Orotava

de la Cruz, see entry), which belonged to La Orotava until 1813.

The town

Although the town has expanded considerably in recent years, it has preserved much of the old town centre with its handsome public buldings. On a stroll through the narrow and sometimes steep streets visitors will come across many old noble mansions with handsome façades and finely decorated balconies.

A good starting-point for a tour of the town centre is the Plaza de la Constitución.

Sights

Plaza de la Constitución

From the flower-decked Plaza de la Constitución there is a superb view over the roofs of the town to the coast which has earned it the name of the "balcony of La Orotava". On the north-east side of the square are the Church and former Monastery of San Agustín, the latter now occupied as a barracks.

Liceo de Taoro

Above the Plaza de la Constitución, reached by way of a small park, is the Liceo de Taoro. Although it is now a private club, visitors are usually allowed into the public rooms (lounges, bar, gaming-rooms, library). From time to time special exhibitions are held here.

Iglesia y Convento de Santo Domingo

Continuing along Carrera de Escultor Estévez and Calle Tomás Zerolo, we pass a number of handsome houses of the

17th–19th c. and come to the Church and former Monastery of
Santo Domingo.

We now go along Calle Viera and Calle Cologán, which lead up
to one of the most impressive churches on the island, the Iglesia
de Nuestra Señora de la Concepción, built between 1768 and
1788 on the foundations of an earlier 16th c. church destroyed
by an earthquake in 1705. With its high dome and two small
towers it is a masterpiece of Baroque architecture, with some
Rococo features. It was declared a national monument in 1948.
Notable features of the interior are the beautiful choir-stalls, the
statues of the Mater Dolorosa and St John by Luján Pérez, the
Baroque retablo of the Virgen de la Concepción and above all the
alabaster and marble High Altar by the Italian sculptor Giuseppe
Gagini, preserved from the earlier church. The Church Treasury
contains a number of liturgical utensils made of precious metals
which originally belonged to St Paul's Cathedral in London.

*Iglesia de Nuestra Señora de la Concepción

A few paces above the church stands the Neo-classical Palacio
Municipal (Town Hall), built between 1871 and 1891.

Palacio Municipal

From here it is a short distance to the Casas de los Balcones in
Calle San Francisco, which are notable for their beautifully
decorated balconies of traditional Canarian type and their
inviting inner courtyards. No. 3, built in 1632, now houses an
embroidery school where work is offered for sale.

*Casas de los Balcones

Some 100 m (110 yd) above the Casas de los Balcones is the
Hospital de la Santísima Trinidad, from the terrace of which
(open to the public) there is a magnificent view of the Orotava

Hospital de la Santísima Trinidad

La Orotava: view of Mount Teide

Iglesia de la Concepción

93

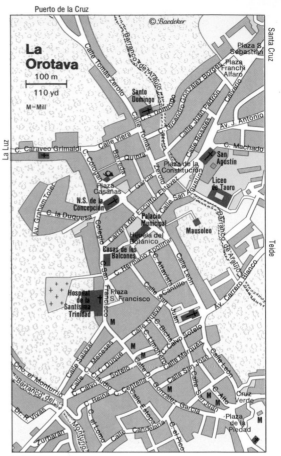

Puerto de la Cruz

La Orotava
100 m
110 yd
M = Mill

La Perdoma

Valley. At the entrance to the hospital is the "revolving cradle" in which foundling children were formerly deposited.

Old mills

The tour can be extended by continuing along Calle San Francisco and up Calle González García, where there are a number of old 17th and 18th c. mills still in operation.

Hijuela del Botánico

The route continues along Calle Hermano Apolinar, which turns off some 50 m (55 yd) below the Hospital de la Santísima Trinidad, to the Hijuela del Botánico (Daughter of the Botanic Garden), behind the Town Hall. This is a branch of the world-famed Botanic Garden between Puerto de la Cruz (see entry), and La Orotava. From here Calle de San Agustín quickly brings us back to the starting-point of the tour in the Plaza de la Constitución.

La Palma (San Miguel de la Palma)   B–D1/2

Area: 728 sq. km (281 sq. miles)
Population: 72,000
Chief place: Santa Cruz de la Palma

La Palma (officially San Miguel de la Palma), the greenest of   Situation
the Canaries, lies some 96 km (60 miles) north-west of Tenerife
between latitude 28°47' and 28°23' N and between longitude
17°59' and 17°41' W.

This heart-shaped island has a maximum length from north to   Topography
south of 47 km (29 miles) and a maximum breadth from east to
west of just under 30 km (19 miles). In the centre of the island
is the Caldera de Taburiente, reaching its highest point in the
Roque de los Muchachos (2426 m (7960 ft)), the second
highest peak in the Canaries. La Palma can thus claim to have
what is, in relation to its area, one of the highest points in the
world. The hills form a ring round the island, with a southward
extension in the narrow ridge of the Cumbre Nueva and its
continuation the Cumbre Vieja. The land falls steeply down to
the coasts, the rugged cliffs interrupted only by a few bays of
black sand. There are numerous springs and perennial streams,
particularly in the north of the island and the Caldera de
Taburiente.

La Palma has continued to be subject to volcanic eruptions into
modern times. The last outbreak (the eruption of Teneguía)
was in October 1971. The huge lava flows in the south of the
island bear witness to former volcanic activity.

An international body has designated La Palma as one of the
three most beautiful islands in the world, and it is easy to see
why. The magnificent scenery and the fascinating vegetation
make an immediate appeal to all who explore the island, either
on foot or by car. And because it lacks any large beaches it has
remained largely unspoiled by mass tourism.

As the most north-westerly island in the Canaries, La Palma is   Climate
more exposed to the influence of the trade winds than the other
islands in the archipelago. Moreover its topography augments
the effects of these winds. The hills form a barrier to the winds
blowing from the north-east, and in a journey across the island
it becomes very evident that the Cumbre Nueva and Cumbre
Vieja mark a climatic boundary: while dense clouds frequently
hang over the north and east of the island the west and south
are usually sunny. Rainfall is high, particularly on the northern
flank of the hills, where the annual figure is over 800 mm
(31 in). Thus with an abundance of ground water and high
rainfall La Palma is the best watered island in the Canaries.

This plentiful water-supply fosters a vegetation of extraordi-   Vegetation
nary luxuriance, and the northern half of the island is covered
with a mantle of greenery and flowers. Almost everywhere La
Palma has preserved its cover of woodland – laurels between
500 and 1000 m (1650 and 3300 ft), pines higher up. At lower
levels the land is intensively cultivated. The dragon tree is found
growing wild here more frequently than on the other Canary
islands.

La Palma

Population

With its 72,000 inhabitants (Palmeros) the island has a population density of 99 to the square kilometre (256 to the square mile). The main concentrations of population are round Santa Cruz in the east and Los Llanos de Aridane and El Paso in the west. In the north of the island there are only a few small settlements; since the main roads are still unsurfaced, they can be reached only on rough and bumpy tracks.

Like Gomera and Hierro, La Palma suffers from a steady drain of population. Although at the beginning of this century the population was still increasing, thereafter, particularly after the Second World War, there was a high emigration rate. Since the beginning of the 1980s, however, there has been a slight increase in population, though this is confined to Santa Cruz and Los Llanos de Aridane. Nevertheless emigration is a decisive factor in the social structure of the island. There are said to be some 40,000 emigrants from La Palma in Venezuela alone. A significant contribution to the economy of the island has been made by emigrants who have returned to La Palma and invested their savings in the island.

Economy

The island's main source of revenue is agriculture. Thanks to La Palma's favourable climatic conditions yields are higher than on the other western Canary islands. The annual banana crop, for example, amounts to 130,000 tonnes, or some 30 per cent of the total production in the Canaries. In view of difficulties in selling bananas there has been a move to switch to other export crops. Round Los Llanos, for example, increasing quantities of tobacco are being grown. Silkworm-rearing has long been practised in the El Paso area, and this is now being developed on an increased scale. Other export crops are almonds, potatoes and wine. Vegetables, fruit and corn are mainly grown for domestic consumption. There is also some stock-farming (mainly goats); fishing is of no economic importance.

The island has only a few small factories processing agricultural produce or producing building materials or craft goods. The only one of any size is a cigarette factory.

The income from tourism is limited. In general the big tour operators do not offer trips to La Palma, and the island is visited mainly by small numbers of independent travellers. Hotel accommodation is available only in Santa Cruz and in the area of Los Llanos de Aridane; even there, fortunately, there are no tower block hotels, only small apartment blocks and guest-houses.

History

Inscriptions dating from pre-Hispanic times have been found on La Palma (particularly in the Cueva de Belmaco, and at the Fuente de la Zara, El Paso and the Roque de Teneguía), but these have not yet been deciphered. We thus know very little about the indigenous inhabitants of the island. They called it Banaohare (Fatherland), and it is believed to have been divided into twelve tribal territories. It was conquered by Spain only in 1492, when Alonso Fernández de Lugo landed at Tazacorte on 29 September, the Feast of St Michael: hence the island's name, San Miguel de la Palma.

Santa Cruz de la Palma ▶

Landscape in the north of La Palma

The Spanish occupation was for the most part achieved without fighting. Only one of the native chieftains, Tanausú, refused to submit; he and his followers entrenched themselves in the Caldera de Taburiente and were overcome only by a ruse. These events are commemorated in the name of the Barranco de las Angustias (Gorge of Anguish). The conquest of the island was completed in May 1493, and it became a direct dependency of the Spanish Crown.

In later centuries La Palma enjoyed considerable prosperity, thanks to the increasing importance of the port of Santa Cruz, which in the 16th and 17th c. was the third largest in the Spanish Empire.

* Santa Cruz de la Palma

General

Santa Cruz de la Palma, the island's capital, lies on the east coast, on the rim of the crater known as La Caldereta. It covers an area of 30 sq. km ($11\frac{1}{2}$ sq. miles) and has a population of 18,500.

The town was founded in 1493 by Alonso Fernández de Lugo and designated from the outset as capital of the island. A few decades later it was granted the privilege, after Antwerp and Seville, of trading with America, and soon developed into one of the leading ports in the Spanish Empire. Not surprisingly, therefore, it became during the 16th c. the target of numerous pirates seeking to gain possession of the city's wealth. In 1553 the town was plundered by a French force under François Le

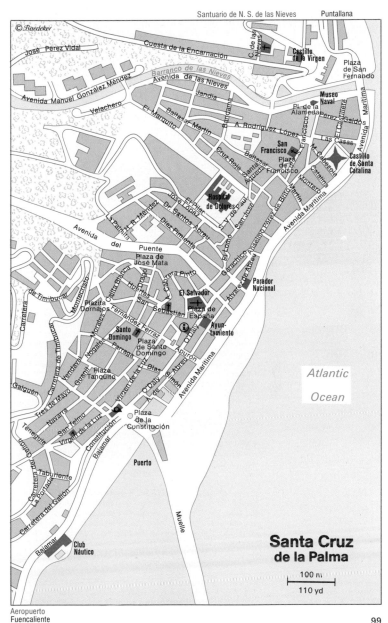

Santuario de N. S. de las Nieves · Puntallana

© Baedeker

José Pérez Vidal

Cuesta de la Encarnación

C. de las Nieves

Castillo de la Virgen

Plaza de San Fernando

Barranco de las Nieves

Avenida de las Nieves

Avenida Manuel González Méndez

Jandia

Museo Naval

Velachero

Baltasar Martín

El Marquito

A. Rodríguez López

Pl. de la Alameda

Pérez Galdós

Las Casas

San Francisco

Avenida Marítima

Cruz Roja

Baltasar

Plaza de S. Francisco

Castillo de Santa Catalina

Santa Azuezca

M. Cabezola

El Pilar

José López

Hospital de Dolores

Catalina

Montero

Dr. Santos Abreu

Díaz Pimienta

San José

Avenida Marítima

A. Padilla · A. F. Méndez

Camino

Garachico

Anselmo Pérez de Brito

Avenida del Puente

Plaza de José Mata

Vera Pinto

Parador Nacional

Álvarez de Abreu

de Timibucar

Carretera

Prado

Calita Blanca

Huertas

El Salvador

San Sebastián

Plaza de España

Plazita Dornajos

Fernández Ferraz

Morales

Nogales

Santo Domingo

Ayuntamiento

Montecristo

O'Daly

Carretera de Timibucar

Vandával

Grumi

Plaza de Santo Domingo

Parraga

Apurón

Galguén

Plaza Tanquito

Virgen de la Luz

Blas

O'Daly

Jo Abreu

Avenida Marítima

Tres de Mayo

Navarra

Limón

de

San Telmo

Atlantic

Ocean

Teneguía

Virgen de la Luz

Plaza de la Constitución

Constitución

Carretera de Gallión

Taburiente

Bajamar

Puerto

La Portada

Carretera del Gallión

Muelle

Bajamar

Club Náutico

Santa Cruz de la Palma

100 m

110 yd

Houses in the Avenida Marítima

Clarc, and some years later the islanders had to repel an attack by Sir Francis Drake. In the 17th c. La Palma became noted for its shipbuilding, and this, together with the American trade, led to the development of other industries including the manufacture of canvas for sails. Merchants from many countries came to Santa Cruz, giving it something of an international atmosphere, and there is still an echo of these times in the many foreign-sounding street names in the town.

With the coming of steamships Santa Cruz declined in importance, but the port still makes a significant contribution to the island's economy.

Far from developing into a mere tourist resort, Santa Cruz has managed to preserve its typical Spanish character. A stay in the island's capital, which still retains its "small-town" atmosphere will appeal to visitors who can forego the usual tourist facilities and luxury shops and restaurants and like to share the life of the ordinary people of the country.

The town

The life of Santa Cruz is centred on its two main streets running parallel to the coast. The principal artery for through traffic is the Avenida Marítima, which has preserved a number of old houses with wooden balconies alongside its imposing modern buildings. Calle O'Daly (also known as Calle Real) is a quieter pedestrian zone with numbers of small shops, cafeterias and restaurants. It runs past the Plaza de España, where the town's most notable buildings are situated.

Ayuntamiento

In the Plaza de España are a number of 18th c. noble mansions and the Ayuntamiento (Town Hall), which dates from the mid 16th c. and which was once the Cardinal's palace. The

Plaza de España, with the Ayuntamiento

Renaissance façade has an arcade of four arches borne on semi-columns surmounted by an upper floor with a range of windows. On the façade are a head of Philip II of Spain (in whose reign the Town Hall was built), the coat of arms of La Palma and the arms of the Austrian Royal House. The door is usually open throughout the day, enabling visitors to see the beautiful panelling of the interior and the murals by Mariano de Cossío (1890–1960) depicting scenes from the life of the islanders.

From the Plaza de España a broad flight of steps leads up to the main doorway of the Iglesia del Salvador, which dates from the second half of the 16th c. Notable features of the three-aisled interior are the coffered wooden ceiling in Mudéjar style and the Gothic vaulting in the sacristy. The altar-piece of the Transfiguration is by the 19th c. Spanish painter Antonio María Esquivel.

Iglesia del Salvador

Following Calle O'Daly and its continuation to the north, we come to the Museo Naval (open Mon.–Fri. 10 a.m.–1 p.m.). This Maritime Museum contains a reproduction of the "Santa María", in which Columbus discovered America in 1493, and models of Columbus's other ships, together with old charts, flags, etc.

Museo Naval

A few paces from the museum, on the Avenida Marítima, stands the Castillo de Santa Catalina, a square structure with corner bastions which was originally built in the 16th c. but much altered in later periods. During the 16th, 17th and 18th c. it served to provide protection against pirates; it now houses the

Castillo de Santa Catalina

Museo de Historia Natural y Etnográfico (open Mon.–Fri. 10 a.m.–1 p.m.), with a small but interesting collection on the history and ethnography of the island.

Parador Nacional

A few hundred metres south of the Castillo, also on the Avenida Marítima, is the Parador Nacional, the best hotel in Santa Cruz, in Spanish Colonial style.

Near by are a number of old houses with fine wooden balconies painted in different colours.

Santuario de Nuestra
Señora de las Nieves

3·5 km (2 miles) west of Santa Cruz, in the outlying district of Las Nieves, is the Santuario de Nuestra Señora de las Nieves, a pilgrimage chapel which houses a terracotta figure of the island's patron saint. The figure, 80 cm (31 in) high, dates from the 14th c. and is the oldest sacred image in the Canaries; it was brought to La Palma from Gran Canaria in the 16th c. It stands on an altar of beaten silver (17th–18th c.). Other notable items in the church are the small Baroque retablos and fine examples of goldsmith's work. Since the end of the 17th c. the Bajada de la Virgen de las Nieves (Descent of the Virgin of the Snows) has been celebrated every five years (next in 1990) with a solemn procession and numerous other events all over the island, lasting a whole month.

**Caldera de Taburiente (Parque Nacional de la Caldera de Taburiente)

The Caldera

The Caldera de Taburiente, declared a National Park in 1954, lies in the exact centre of the island. With a circumference of 28 km (17 miles) and a maximum diameter of almost 9 km (5½ miles), it is one of the world's largest volcanic craters. The geological term caldera (English cauldron), applied to an unusually broad crater which has been enlarged by collapse or erosion, was originally derived from the Caldera de Taburiente. The highest point on the rim of the crater is the Roque de los Muchachos (2426 m (7960 ft)).

Barranco de las Angustias

The Caldera de Taburiente area is well supplied with water and has accordingly been much eroded. The water is drained by the Barranco de las Angustias (Gorge of Anguish), forming numerous waterfalls up to 50 m (165 ft) high. This was the last refuge of the indigenous inhabitants during the Spanish conquest.

Roque Idafe

Near the Barranco de las Angustias, on the western rim of the caldera, is the Roque Idafe, a monolithic basalt column which the natives held to be sacred.

La Cumbrecita

Those who do not feel inclined for a long walk in the National Park can get a fascinating view of the Caldera de Taburiente from La Cumbrecita (1833 m (6014 ft)), a viewpoint which can be reached by car on a narrow asphalted road. It offers an impressive prospect of the sheer rock walls of the caldera, but the view into the crater bottom is obstructed by the tall trees.

There is an even better view from the Mirador de las Chozas, reached from La Cumbrecita on a forest track negotiable by cars. This also makes a rewarding walk (about 1 km (¾ mile)), with a succession of fantastic views of the caldera.

Observatorio de Astrofísica

Near the Roque de los Muchachos is an astrophysical

La Cumbrecita: view into the Caldera de Taburiente

Observatorio de Astrofísica

observatory opened in 1985. It is reached on a new track which runs from Miranda (4 km (2½ miles) north of Santa Cruz) via Mirca, on the edge of the Los Andenes range, to the Roque de los Muchachos. A number of different countries contributed to the establishment of the observatory, one of the most important of its kind in the world. The choice fell on this site because of the favourable climatic conditions on the summit of La Palma's highest peak: at this height there are many cloudless nights and the air is particularly clear. The various countries involved in the project are responsible for the installation, maintenance and use of the instruments. Thus the Swedes, for example, built a 15 m (50 ft) high "sun tower" equipped with instruments and apparatus for the observation of the sun.

Other sights on La Palma

The following descriptions of other features of interest on La Palma are so arranged as to form possible round trips from Santa Cruz. Visitors who want to get even a brief impression of the whole of the island should allow at least two days. One day could be devoted to the exploration of the northern half of the island, returning to Santa Cruz by way of El Paso and the Túnel de la Cumbre. A drive round the southern part of the island should begin with a visit to the viewpoint of La Cumbrecita (p. 102); but since clouds begin to form there in the course of the morning a very early start is advisable. Thereafter the route from El Paso onwards should be followed.

Puntallana

From Santa Cruz the road goes north, with numerous bends, to Puntallana (10 km (6 miles)), which has a 16th c. parish church, the Iglesia de San Juan, with a 16th c. figure of St John (Flemish work).
Beyond Puntallana the landscape becomes even more fertile and greener, if that is possible.

Cubo de la Galga

Soon after the village of La Galga a road branches off on the left, signposted to the hill forest of Cubo de la Galga. Although the first stretch is asphalted, the road soon degenerates into a narrow track unsuitable for cars.

Mirador de San Bartolomé

From the Mirador de San Bartolomé, near the Ermita de San Bartolomé in La Galga, there is a fine general view of the country, deeply slashed by *barrancos* (gorges).

San Andrés y Sauces

28 km (17 miles) from Santa Cruz the road comes to San Andrés y Sauces, the principal agricultural and commercial centre in the north of the island. A narrow road runs up through terraced banana plantations to San Andrés.
The parish church of Los Sauces, on the main road, contains a figure of Nuestra Señora de Montserrat.
Continuing on the main road, we come in 1·5 km (1 mile) to a side road on the left leading to the dense woodland (laurels and ferns) of Los Tilos, which has something of the aspect of a primaeval forest. To prevent any further destruction of the environment here the area is under UNESCO protection.

Barlovento

Barlovento, at the north-east corner of La Palma, lies in an intensively cultivated area. It has a 17th c. church, the Iglesia de Nuestra Señora del Rosario.

Terraced banana groves in the north of La Palma

1 km ($\frac{3}{4}$ mile) beyond Barlovento a narrow road on the left leads to the Laguna de Barlovento, the largest artificial lake (reservoir) on the island.

The vegetation now changes. The road traverses an area densely overgrown with scrub, which soon gives place to pine woods.

At the spring of Las Mimbreras is a picnic spot, with wooden tables and benches and toilet facilities. **Fuente Las Mimbreras**

The villages in the northern part of the island are of so little economic importance or tourist interest that it has not been thought necessary to provide a modern road system. However, the forest track which begins here is perfectly practicable for cars, and there is even the occasional bus. Visitors may well feel themselves on the frontier of civilization as they jolt their way along the bumpy track through a roughly hewn and unlighted tunnel. They will seldom meet another car, though the way may be blocked from time to time by a herd of goats.

13 km (8 miles) beyond Las Mimbreras we reach the village of Roque Faro, with a bar which offers the possibility of refreshment.

Soon after this a footpath (10 minutes) branches off on the left **Fuente de la Zarza**
to the prehistoric inscriptions at the Fuente de la Zarza (Spring of the Brambles). There are other large petroglyphs near by in the little Baranquillo (Gorge) de la Zarza and the Caldera de Agua.

Continuing west on the main road, we come to Llano Negro **Garafía**
(rock inscriptions at the Fuente Secreta), where the road

105

diverges to the remote little settlement of Garafía. From this point the road is again asphalted.

Puntagorda

The road continues past vineyard-covered slopes and other intensively cultivated land and in 8 km (5 miles) reaches Puntagorda. To get some impression of rural life in this area, leave the main road at the first turning for Puntagorda and drive through the long straggling village, one of the most beautiful on the island. The villagers live by growing bananas, potatoes, almonds and flowers. From the end of the village the by-road continues in a wide arc to rejoin the main road.

°Mirador El Time

One of the finest viewpoints on La Palma is the Mirador El Time (594 m (1949 ft)), which affords a breath-taking prospect of the west coast, the Barranco de las Angustias and the wide Aridane Plain, with banana plantations everywhere.
From here the road winds its way down the wall of the Barranco de las Angustias and then climbs again.

Tazacorte

7 km (4¼ miles) beyond the Mirador El Time a road goes off on the right to the village of Tazacorte, which lives by banana-growing and fishing. There are a number of 16th c. noble mansions in the main street.

Puerto de Tazacorte

3 km (2 miles) north of Tazacorte lies Puerto de Tazacorte, where the Spaniards landed in 1492. The numerous fishing-boats and the beach of volcanic sand make a picturesque backdrop. On the beach are a number of small fish restaurants.

°Cueva Bonita

From Puerto de Tazacorte there is an attractive boat trip to the

Mirador El Time: view of the Aridane Plain

Puerto de Tazacorte

Cueva Bonita, 6 km (4 miles) to the north-west. This "Beautiful Cave" with its fascinating effects of light and colour can be reached only by boat.

From Tazacorte the route continues through luxuriant banana plantations to Puerto Naos, which is noted for its beach, the most popular on the island. As a result there has been a considerable increase in the tourist trade in recent years. Attempts are being made to attract more foreign visitors, as witness the small seafront promenade, with a café and some other tourist attractions. The building boom is still on a very limited scale, with the development consisting mainly of small apartment blocks. One unsightly feature is a large ruined building at the south end of the beach.

Puerto Naos

From Puerto Naos a narrow road continues south to Charco Verde, which also offers reasonably good bathing.

Charco Verde

To continue the circuit of the island we must now return on the same road to Los Llanos de Aridane, the island's second largest town (pop. 16,500), in the Aridane Valley. The area round Los Llanos is the largest banana-growing region on La Palma. In view of the possible dangers of this monoculture of bananas there has been a trend in recent years towards diversification by introducing the growing of avocados.
In the centre of the little town stands the Iglesia de Nuestra Señora de los Remedios (1507), which has a 16th c. Flemish figure of the Virgin, patroness of the town.

Los Llanos de Aridane

5 km (3 miles) east of Los Llanos is El Paso, the only place in

El Paso

Puerto Naos

the Canaries where silkworms are still reared and silk is produced. Contributions are also made to the modest prosperity of the place by the growing of tobacco and the manufacture of cigarettes and cigars.

Fuencaliente

35 km (22 miles) from El Paso we come to Fuencaliente, the most southerly settlement on the island. It gets its name (hot spring) from a sulphurous spring which is said to have existed here in the past. The town is famed for its wine (Malvasía). But it was something very different that made its name known beyond the bounds of the Canaries – the nearby volcano of Teneguía.

*Volcan de Teneguía

A few kilometres south of Fuencaliente, on the slopes of the old volcano of San Antonio (657 m (2156 ft)), a series of continuous seismic movements was followed on 26 October 1971 by a volcanic eruption, with further eruptions continuing until 22 November. The masses of ash and lava expelled during the eruptions formed a new volcanic cone, the Volcán de Teneguía (439 m (1440 ft)). The volcano is no longer active, but vapours still emerge from cracks in the crater bottom. The best view of Teneguía is to be had from the southern rim of the San Antonio crater, which can be reached after a short walk.

Cueva de Belmaco

At the village of Tigalate the road to Santa Cruz forks. The lower road, to the east, comes soon after km 8 to the Cueva de Belmaco, with prehistoric rock inscriptions (not yet deciphered).

Mazo

3 km (2 miles) north of the Cueva de Belmaco lies the village

of Mazo, with the Iglesia de San Blás, which has a fine High Altar and a number of 16th c. statues. Many visitors come here, however, not so much for the sake of the church as for the potters' workshop housed in an old mill, El Molino. Pottery is made here by traditional native methods (without the use of a wheel) and decorated with traditional patterns. Attached to the workshop is a small exhibition of pre-Hispanic objects.

The last places before Santa Cruz are Breña Baja and Breña Alta. In the San Isidro district, above the main road, can be seen a botanical curiosity in the form of twin dragon trees (the Dragos Gemelos).
To the north, in Breña Alta, stands the Iglesia de San Pedro, founded in the 16th c. but much altered in later times. The font and the figure of Nuestra Señora del Socorro date from the period of the Spanish conquest.
From the Mirador de la Concepción, at the north end of Breña Alta, there are magnificent views of the Las Breñas Valley and Santa Cruz.

Breña Baja/Breña Alta

---

*Las Montañas de Anaga   A/B9–11

The Montañas de Anaga (Anaga Hills) occupy the whole of the north-eastern tip of Tenerife. On the south side of this rugged range of hills is the La Laguna Plateau.

Situation

The Anaga range, running from north-east to south-west, consists of a series of peaks of about 1000 m (3300 ft), the highest of which is Taborno (1024 m (3360 ft)). The hills fall steeply down on both sides, slashed here and there by deep gorges (*barrancos*).
Geologically, the Anaga Hills are one of the oldest parts of the island, as is shown by the topography of the area. In the course of many million years the original lava flows have been eroded away, leaving only the harder rocks (basalt). As a result the hills as we see them today are rugged and bizarrely shaped, looking from a distance forbidding and inaccessible. This first impression, however, is modified when, closer up, the slopes are seen to be covered with luxuriant green. Since the Anaga Hills lie within the area of influence of the north-eastern trade winds, and accordingly are frequently shrouded in mist, they are well provided with water. At lower and medium heights there are dense forests of laurels, which at higher levels give place to heath and laurel scrub.
Only part of the range is well served by roads. A good road runs from La Laguna via Mercedes and along the crest of the hills to the viewpoint of El Bailadero, from which there are roads leading north to Taganana and south to San Andrés. The hill villages in the eastern part of the peninsula can also be reached by road, but it is not possible to drive round Tenerife's north-eastern tip, and many of the farms are still well off any road accessible to cars. There are a number of bays with beaches which can only be reached by sea.

Topography

These conditions naturally have their effect on the population of the area. Some of the inhabitants have abandoned their modest holdings to seek employment in the towns; others

Population

remain, living without the amenities of modern civilization in their little cottages. They exist on the produce of their small terraced fields; most of them also keep goats, which can be seen everywhere grazing on the steep hillsides.

Viewpoints

For visitors whose time is limited the best plan is to take the ridge road which runs north-east from La Laguna and at El Bailadero turn south for San Andrés. On this route there are numerous viewpoints affording extensive panoramas over the countryside.

Mirador de Jardina

Shortly after Las Mercedes the road reaches the Mirador de Jardina, from which there is a fine prospect of the La Laguna Plateau. As the name of the viewpoint indicates, the countryside here is like a garden, with green hills and the outlying districts of the town of La Laguna in the background.

Cruz del Carmen

The road now winds its way up through the Las Mercedes Forest to the Cruz del Carmen (920 m (3019 ft)). At this viewpoint there is a chapel dating from the early 17th c. with a much-venerated figure of Nuestra Señora de las Mercedes. There is a picnic place and also a restaurant.

Mirador Pico del Inglés

The Mirador Pico del Inglés offers what is perhaps the best panoramic view of the Anaga Hills. The prospect also extends to Mount Teide, Santa Cruz and in clear weather the island of Gran Canaria.

View from the Mirador de Jardina

The Mirador del Bailadero is the last viewpoint on the ridge road. One looks down on both flanks of the range, with a glimpse, far below to the south, of the little town of San Andrés (see entry), backed by the brilliant blue of the sea. There are two modest bars offering the possibility of refreshment.

Mirador del Bailadero

Sights

Soon after the village of Las Mercedes the ridge road comes to an important ecological feature of Tenerife – the Bosque de las Mercedes, a "primaeval forest" of laurels which extends up to the higher levels of the range.

Bosque de las Mercedes

To the east of Punta del Hidalgo is the troglodytic village of Chinamada (alt. 614 m (2015 ft)), its few small houses scattered over the rolling countryside. At first glance the houses of Chinamada look little different from those of other villages; it is only on a closer view that they are seen to be hewn from the rock of the hillsides. These cave dwellings may be anything up to 20 sq. m (215 sq. ft) in size and, as fitted out and furnished by their occupants, can be surprisingly comfortable.

** Chinamada

A walk which takes in Chinamada is described below; the village still cannot be reached by car.

From the Mirador del Bailadero a road winds its way down, with never-ending bends, to Taganana, near the north coast. As it approaches Taganana there are charming views of this picturesque little village. Sugar-cane was formerly grown here, but the area is now known for its excellent wine.

Taganana

There are bathing beaches below Taganana, at Playa de San Roque and Playa de Benijo.

On the coast 3 km (2 miles) north-east of Taganana lies the village of Almáciga, which has a 17th c. chapel dedicated to the Virgen de Begoña, patroness of the Basque country.

Almáciga

Walks in the Anaga Hills

The best way of getting to know the lonely and unspoiled country of the Anaga Hills is on foot. Along the ridge road, on both sides, there are signposts indicating possible walks. The walks described below are waymarked. For fuller information consult the green ICONA map (Zone 1), obtainable from tourist information offices (see Practical Information – Information).

From the Cabezo del Tejo viewpoint (1·5 km (1 mile) south of El Draguillo) the route runs east by way of the village of Chamorga to the Faro de Anaga (lighthouse). It then continues to the hamlet of Las Palmas and runs parallel with the coast to Almáciga. This walk takes 5–6 hours; apart from the short climb to the lighthouse it follows a fairly level course.

Cabezo del Tejo–Faro de Anaga–Almáciga

This circuit begins at the picnic spot 2 km (1¼ miles) west of El Bailadero. After a steep climb to Mount Chinobre (910 m (2986 ft)) the route continues to Mount Anambro (864 m (2835 ft)) and then descends to the Cabezo del Tejo viewpoint

Parque Forestal de Anaga–Chinobre–Anambro–Cabezo del Tejo–Parque Forestal de Anaga

(670 m (2198 ft)). The return route is on the Pista Forestal. Time 1½ hours.

El Bailadero–Almáciga

This short walk from the El Bailadero viewpoint to Almáciga takes about an hour and affords a succession of magnificent views of the rugged hills.

Casa Forestal–Camino de las Vueltas–Taganana

From the Casa Forestal (forestry house) follow the Camino de las Vueltas. Until the early 1960s this winding track was the only way to get to Taganana. Time about 1 hour.

Las Carboneras–Chinamada–Punta del Hidalgo

This walk, which passes the troglodytic village of Chinamada (above), takes about 3 hours. The best starting-point is the village of Las Carboneras. It can, of course, be done in the reverse direction, but this is considerably more strenuous, with some steep climbing.

Los Cristianos   D7

Altitude: sea-level
Population: 2500

Situation and characteristics

Los Cristianos lies in a sheltered bay on the south coast of Tenerife, 15 km (9 miles) west of the Reina Sofia Airport. Thanks to its beautiful climate, with almost perpetual sunshine, this little fishing village has developed in the last ten years or so into a popular holiday resort. New building is still going on, and Los Cristianos is gradually merging with the hotel settlement of Playa de las Américas (see entry).

The town

Approaching Los Cristianos, the visitor sees at first only huge apartment blocks and hotels, laid out on wide new streets. Since it hardly ever rains here and the surrounding country is barren and desolate, it seems at first sight more like a building site than an attractive holiday resort. This first impression, however, is deceptive. The hotels and bungalows are set in luxuriant gardens and most of the streets are lined by palms. Moreover, unlike many resorts in the Canaries, Los Cristianos has preserved the original nucleus of the town. This contains no major buildings, but the little pedestrian zone with its shops and restaurants and the plaza near the harbour have an atmosphere all their own. Sitting in one of the cafés, visitors soon forget the passage of time, for there is always something to see – the arrival or departure of the Gomera ferry, the fishermen returning with their catch, the elegant yachts, and even the dogs which are an essential element in the street scene.

The beach

In contrast to other coastal towns on Tenerife, Los Cristianos has a beach of some size (400 m (440 yd) long and up to 110 m (120 yd) wide). Along the beach extends a spacious paved promenade.

Chayofa

4 km (2½ miles) north of Los Cristianos is Chayofa, one of the most attractive holiday villages on the island, with many comfortable vacation homes built by well-to-do European

Los Cristianos

visitors. The houses are surrounded by luxuriant gardens which form a striking contrast to the bare surrounding hills. Since Chayofa is considerably higher than Los Cristianos it is usually cooler and more agreeable here than in the coastal resort.

Los Gigantes

See Puerto de Santiago

Los Realejos   B8

Altitude: 260–420 m (850–1380 ft)
Population (district): 26,000

Los Realejos, 5 km (3 miles) west of Puerto de la Cruz, consists of a higher part, Realejo Alto, and a lower part, Realejo Viejo. It was here that the last Guanche chiefs submitted to the Spanish conquerors in 1496.

The town's main source of income is agriculture, but the holiday villages of La Romántica I and II are also within its territory.

Situation and characteristics

The houses of the town extend up the slopes of the hill, surrounded by luxuriant banana plantations. There are three notable churches.

The town

113

The oldest church on Tenerife is the Iglesia de Santiago in Realejo Alto, built in 1498, with additions in later centuries. The tower (18th c.) contains a bell presented by Ferdinand of Aragon (1452–1516) and Isabella of Castile (1451–1504). Higher up in Realejo Alto stands the Iglesia de Nuestra Señora del Carmen. In front of it can be seen a statue of the writer and historian José de Viera y Clavijo (1731–1812), who was born in Los Realejos.

The Iglesia de Nuestra Señora de la Concepción in Realejo Bajo has a fine 17th c. wood altar and a jasper font.

La Romántica

Near the rocky coast a few kilometres east of Los Realejos lie the holiday developments of Romántica I and II. The scenery is certainly romantic, though the effect is slightly soiled by a number of modern tower blocks. Most of the bungalows and apartments have views of the bizarrely shaped rocks along the coast and the ever restless sea. Because of the heavy surf bathing is usually possible only in the swimming-pool. Romántica II is particularly trim, no doubt because many of the houses are privately owned.

La Guancha

10 km (6 miles) west of Los Realejos is the village of La Guancha, formerly famed for its pottery. There is now a craft school which has established a considerable reputation. The village church, which dates from the 17th c., is notable for its fine woodcarving and its Baroque altar.

Los Roques

See Caldera de las Cañadas

Los Silos   B7

Altitude: 111 m (364 ft)
Population (district): 5200

Situation and characteristics

Los Silos lies in the north-west of Tenerife, 6 km (3½ miles) west of Garachico and 2 km (1¼ miles) from the coast. It was originally planned to establish a holiday centre here, but the project never got past the early stages. As a result the seawater swimming-pool near the village is used almost exclusively by local people.

The village

The modest houses of the village cluster round an attractive shady plaza and a typical village church. The church contains a 17th c. figure of the Cristo de la Misericordia which is attributed to Juan de Mesa.

Masca

See Teno Hills

Orotava Valley

See Valle de la Orotava

**Parque Nacional del Teide   C7/8

The Parque Nacional del Teide (Teide National Park), in the centre of Tenerife, is a gigantic lunar landscape which every visitor should see. Established in 1954, it was Spain's third National Park. It is bounded on the north by Mount Teide (see entry) and on the south-east and west by the steep rock walls of the Caldera de las Cañadas (see entry). The whole area of the park (13,500 hectares (33,300 acres)) lies above 2000 m (6560 ft).

Situation and topography

Climatic conditions in the National Park are very different from those prevailing in the rest of the island. The strong sunlight produces unusually high daytime temperatures (in summer up to 40 °C (104 °F)), which fall sharply at night. The relative humidity of the air is low (under 50 per cent, in summer sometimes below 25 per cent). The annual precipitation is 400 mm

Climate

The bizarre lunar landscape of the Teide National Park

115

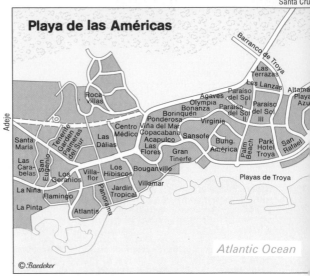

Santa Cru

Playa de las Américas

Atlantic Ocean

© Baedeker

(16 in), mostly in the form of snow during the winter months.

Flora

Considering the altitude and the unfavourable soil conditions in the National Park, its flora is remarkably rich. Some forty-five species grow here, including some which are found only in this area.

The commonest shrubs on the great expanses of pumice and volcanic detritus are the Teide broom (*Spartocytisus supranubius*), with white and pink flowers, and the yellow-flowered *Adenocarpus viscosus*. With a little luck you may find (perhaps near the Parador Nacional) one of the most striking plants in the Canaries, *taginaste rojo* (*Echium wildpretii*), with flower-bearing stalks up to 2 m (nearly 7 ft) high. Among other species common here are the *hierba pajonera* (*Descourainia bourgaeana*; yellow flowers), the Teide daisy (*Argyranthemum teneriffae*; white flowers) and the stock-like *alhelí de las Cañadas* (*Cheiranthus scoparius*; crimson flowers). It is only very rarely and in the highest regions of the Montaña Blanca and Mount Teide that the Teide violet (*Viola cheiranthifolia*) discovered by Alexander von Humboldt can still be found.

Fauna

The fauna shows less variety. Apart from small numbers of cats and rabbits which have gone wild and the Canary lizard there are only various species of birds (ravens, partridges, rock doves, Canary chaffinches, etc.). The insects are well represented, with some 400 species, predominantly endemic.

Centro de Visitantes (Visitor Centre)

Opening times:
daily 9 a.m.–4 p.m.

Further information about the Parque Nacional del Teide can be obtained in the Centro de Visitantes (Visitor Centre) at El

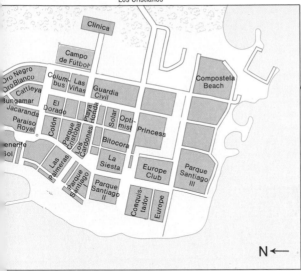

Los Cristianos

N ←

Portillo. Graphic displays show the National Parks in the Canaries and illustrate the formation of the Caldera de las Cañadas. There are also specimens of various volcanic rocks and examples of typical forms taken by lava after hardening.

Displays which can be illuminated by pressing a button introduce visitors to the flora and fauna of the Teide National Park.

All labels and displays are in Spanish, but it is sometimes possible to join a conducted party with explanations in English. Informative material and books can be bought at the sales counter on the ground floor. Video presentations are given in the basement (hourly, on the hour).

Pico de Teide

See Teide

Playa de las Américas   D7

Altitude: sea-level

Playa de las Américas, on the south coast of Tenerife, combines with Los Cristianos (see entry), 3 km (2 miles) away, to form the largest holiday complex in the south of the island. The bed capacity of the joint resort, at present 36,000, is due to be increased to 50,000.

Situation and characteristics

Playa de las Américas is a brand-new tourist resort, created

The resort

from scratch in 1966; there was no older settlement on the site. It is now a place of broad palm-fringed streets, comfortable hotels, huge apartment blocks and countless restaurants, cafés and shops.

Bathing facilities are limited. There are only three small coves with beaches of brownish-black sand, on which, during the main winter season, it is necessary to book your place early in the day. In order to make good the deficiency a new beach (Las Vistas) is being created between Playa de la Américas and Los Cristianos.

Aguapark Octopus

To increase the leisure facilities of Playa de las Américas an oasis of blue-green water, the Aguapark Octopus, has been created in the barren landscape to the north of the resort (2 km (1¼ miles) from the town centre). Here visitors can swim and enjoy a variety of water sports. The principal attractions are the huge water-chute and the two fast-water runs. There are free bus services from Playa de la Américas, and excursions to the Aguapark are run from as far afield as the north of the island.

Opening times:
daily 10 a.m.–6 p.m.

Puerto de la Cruz   B8

Altitude: sea-level
Population: 40,000

Puerto de la Cruz lies in the north of Tenerife, at the mouth of the celebrated Orotava Valley. Within a few decades it has passed through a lightning course of development, from a small fishing town to an internationally known tourist resort, the largest on Tenerife. With its extensive range of leisure and recreational facilities it is an ideal holiday place for those who like variety and want beautiful scenery but do not necessarily expect a brilliantly blue sky every day – for sometimes, particularly in winter, the sun is concealed behind heavy cloud.

Situation and characteristics

Puerto de la Cruz was founded at the beginning of the 17th c. as the port for La Orotava (see entry) and was originally known as Puerto de la Orotava. Most of the wine produced on Tenerife was shipped from here.

The development into a modern tourist metropolis began at the end of the 19th c., when well-to-do British people began to discover its attractions and the first guest-houses and hotels, of modest size, were built. The real tourist boom began only in the mid 20th c.

History

Unlike other holiday towns in the Canaries, Puerto de la Cruz has contrived to preserve its own distinctive atmosphere. Here visitors will find attractive old houses in traditional Canarian style, shady squares which, at least at week-ends, are not frequented solely by tourists, and a seafront promenade of some architectural distinction. These factors, together with the agreeable climate and the luxuriant vegetation it fosters, make it easy to forget that Puerto de la Cruz lies on a rocky and

·The town

◄ *Seafront promenade, with Teide in background*

119

Lido San Telmo

inhospitable coast and has only small beaches of black sand. To make good this last deficiency it is planned to improve the stretch of coast between the Castillo de San Felipe and the Punta Brava district and to build an artificial reef to shelter it.

Sights in the central area

The features described in this section can be seen on a short tour of the town, taking them in the order indicated.

****Lido San Telmo/
Costa de Martiánez**

The main attractions for holiday-makers are undoubtedly the bathing centre, designed by the Lanzarote architect César Manrique and completed in 1977, and the seafront promenade on the Avenida de Colón. Within the complex of the Lido San Telmo, or Costa de Martiánez as this stretch of coast is also known, are a large artificial lake with islands of lava rock and several smaller swimming-pools. One of the lava islands, to the great delight of the children, suddenly transforms itself at intervals into a huge fountain. A southern air is given to the complex by palms, exotic flowers and beautiful green lawns.
For those who not feel inclined to bathe, the promenade along the Avenida de Colón offers plenty of shady spots from which to observe the busy activity round the sales kiosks and stalls and the comings and goings of visitors.

Capilla San Telmo

The Chapel of San Telmo seems entirely at home on the seafront promenade. Built in 1626 by seamen and fishermen for their patron saint San Telmo (St Elmo), it was badly damaged by fire in 1778 and by a storm in 1826, and thereafter was restored. A thorough restoration was carried out in 1968. The much-revered figure of San Pedro González Telmo was destroyed in the 1778 fire; the present statue dates from 1783. The coats of arms behind the altar show the emblems of the Dominicans and of seamen.

The Plaza de los Reyes Católicos, adjoining the Chapel of San Telmo, is named after the Catholic Monarch, Ferdinand of Aragon (1452–1516) and his wife Isabella of Castile (1451–1504), during whose reign Tenerife was conquered by Spain. In the centre of the square is a bust of Francisco de Miranda (1750–1816), who fought for the independence of Venezuela from Spain. His parents came from Puerto de la Cruz (see Casa de Miranda).

Plaza de los
Reyes Católicos

The seafront promenade leads to the little square known as the Punta del Viento, from which there are fine views of the Lido San Telmo and the dark rocky coast, often lashed by heavy surf.

Punta del Viento

Continuing along Calle Quintana (pedestrian zone), we come to the Plaza de la Iglesia, in which, surrounded by palms and flower-beds, stands the Iglesia de Nuestra Señora de la Peña de Francia, the town's most important church, built in the early 17th c. It has an ornate Baroque retablo by Luis de la Cruz, and among its other treasures are a number of figures of Christ, the Virgin and saints: the Cristo del Gran Poder, by an unknown 18th c. sculptor, the 17th c. Virgen del Rosario and the Virgen de los Dolores and Santo Domingo, both by Luján Pérez.

Iglesia de Nuestra Señora
de la Peña de Francia

From the next intersection along Calle Quintana there is a fine view of the Casino Taoro on the hill above the town. This gaming casino, set in beautiful grounds, was formerly a hotel.

Casino Taoro

We now turn into Calle de Agustín de Béthencourt, which leads to Calle Iriarte, from which it is only a few paces to the Casa Iriarte in Calle San Juan. With beautiful carved balconies this old noble mansion gives an excellent impression of traditional Canarian architecture. It now houses showrooms for the sale of embroidery and souvenirs. Visitors can also get some idea of the history of Puerto de la Cruz from the pictures on display here; there is a small shipping museum. Every visitor should at least glance into the beautiful inner courtyard.

Casa Iriarte

Near here is the Plaza del Charco, shaded by tall Indian laurels, the hub of the town's life and a meeting-place for both visitors and locals. The laurels were first brought to Puerto de la Cruz in 1852 and soon spread widely over the island.

Plaza del Charco

Below the Plaza del Charco lies the harbour, now used only by a few fishermen. The two piers are the scene of bustling activity, particularly in the early morning. The shorter of the two was built in 1720, the other more than a century later.

Puerto Pesquero

The oldest surviving building in Puerto de la Cruz is the Real Aduana, on the harbour, which served as the Custom House from 1706 to 1833. Embroidery and other souvenirs are now sold here; and in addition "Expo Tenerife", a multivision show on the history of the Canaries, runs throughout the day. (Open daily 9.40 a.m.–1 p.m. and 3–6 p.m., Expo Tenerife half-hourly 10 a.m.–1 p.m. and 4–7 p.m.)

Casa de la Real Aduana

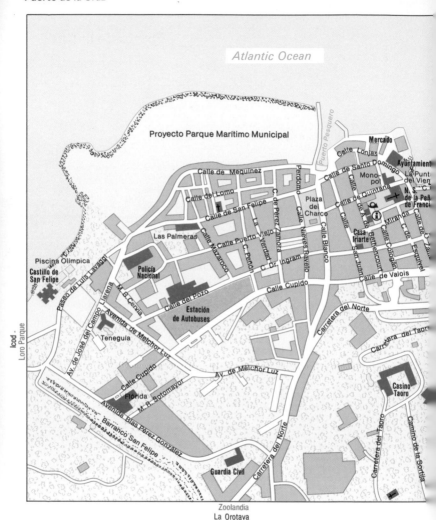

Zoolandia
La Orotava

Casa de Miranda	The Casa de Miranda, in Calle Santo Domingo, was built in 1730. It is said to have belonged to the Miranda family, who later emigrated to Venezuela (see Plaza de los Reyes Católicos).
Mercado	The tour of Puerto de la Cruz can be concluded by a stroll through the market, which lies close to the Casa Miranda. Among the articles offered for sale are clothing, leather goods and souvenirs.

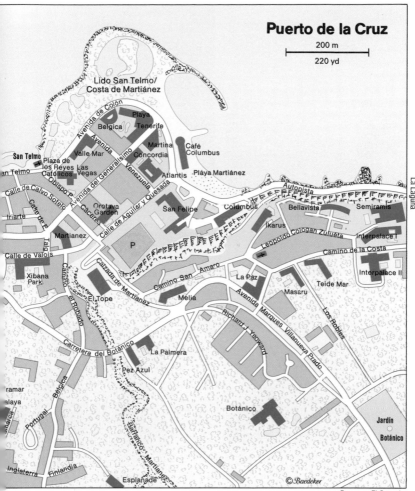

Puerto de la Cruz

200 m
220 yd

Lido San Telmo/
Costa de Martiánez

Playa
Tenerife

Belgica

Avenida de Colón

Avenida

Martina
Concordia

Valle Mar

Café
Columbus

San Telmo
Plaza de
los Reyes Las
Católicos Vegas

an Telmo

Obispo P.

Venezuela

Avenida del Generalísimo

Atlantis

Playa Martiánez

Calle de Calvo Sotelo

Orotava
Garden

Autopista

Cáceres

Calle de E.

Iriarte

Calle de Aguilar y Quesada

San Felipe

Columbus

Bellavista

Semiramis

Martianez

P

Ikarus

Leopoldo Cologan Zulueta

Interpalace I

Calle de Valois

Camino de la Costa

Xibana
Park

Calzada de Martiánez

Camino San Amaro

La Paz

Interpalace II

Camino el Robado

El Tope

Mélia

Avenida Marques Villanueva Prado

Teide Mar

Masaru

Los Robles

Calle de Talja

Carretera del Botánico

La Palmera

Richard J. Yeoward

Bélgica

Pez Azul

ramar
alaya

Portugal

Barranco Martianez

Botánico

Jardín

Botánico

Inglaterra Finlandia

Esplanade

© Baedeker

Santa Cruz
La Laguna

Bananera El Guanche
La Orotava, Santa Cruz

**Jardín Botánico

The Botanic Garden (officially the Jardín de Aclimatación de la
Orotava) was established by King Charles III of Spain (1716–
88) in order to accustom tropical plants to a more temperate
climate. The plants were successfully acclimatized to Tenerife,
but the second part of the plan – to go on from there to
accustom the plants to the climate of mainland Spain – was a
failure. Within an area of only 2·5 hectares (6 acres) the Botanic

Situation:
2 km (1¼ miles) SE on
Carretera del Botánico

Opening times:
daily 9 a.m.–6 p.m.

123

Puerto de la Cruz

Capilla de San Telmo

Church of Nuestra Señora de la Peña de Francia

Jardín Botánico

Zoolandia

Garden contains more than 200 species of plants and trees from all over the world, including breadfruit trees, cinnamon trees, pepper trees, coffee plants, mangoes and tulip trees; various species of orchids are grown in hothouses and variety is provided by a small water-lily pond in the upper part of the gardens and a fountain.

Continuing on the road beyond the Botanic Garden, we come in 2 km (1¼ miles) to the celebrated Mirador Humboldt. Inscribed on the commemorative stone is a remark by Alexander von Humboldt on the beauty of the Orotava Valley.

Mirador Humboldt

Bananera El Guanche

At the Bananera El Guanche visitors can learn about the cultivation and processing of the banana. A short video film and a series of signs explain the various stages of development of the banana plants. In the rear part of the area there is a short circular route going past other exotic plants of economic importance, including sugar-cane, coffee, avocados and pawpaws. A brochure given to visitors with the admission ticket provides fuller information about methods of cultivation and the importance of the banana to the economy of the Canaries.
(There is a free bus service from Playa Martiánez/Café Columbus.)

Situation:
3 km (2 miles) SE

Opening times:
daily 8.30 a.m.–6.15 p.m.

Zoolandia

Zoolandia, the first zoo in the Canaries, was opened in the autumn of 1986. In this attractive subtropical park, with an area of only 1·5 hectares (3¾ acres), bears, lions, tigers, chimpanzees, reptiles and various species of birds are kept in enclosures, some of which are quite small. The zoo will appeal particularly to children, for whom the pony rides offer an additional attraction.
(Free bus service from Playa Martiánez/Café Columbus.)

Situation:
4 km (2½ miles) S, on motorway to Santa Cruz, La Orotava turn-off

Opening times:
daily 9 a.m.–6 p.m.

Castillo de San Felipe

This little castle is named after King Philip IV (1621–65), who ordered the foundation of the town of La Orotava and the port of Puerto de la Orotava (now Puerto de la Cruz). The Castillo de San Felipe, built in the early 17th c., is the only building in the Canaries in pure Spanish Colonial style. It now houses a restaurant.
(Free bus service from Playa Martiánaz/Café Columbus.)

Situation:
1 km (¾ mile) W, on Paseo de Luis Lavaggi

Loro Parque (Parrot Park)

A visit to the Parrot Park would be worth while if only for the sake of seeing the extensive and carefully tended grounds, which cover an area of over 5 hectares (12½ acres). Here, in a setting of tropical and subtropical plants, visitors can see more than 200 out of the world's 335 known species of parrots. Since it is one of the objectives of the Loro Parque to breed

Situation:
3 km (2 miles) W, in Punta Brava district

Loro Parque

Parrot Park
Puerto de la Cruz

Entrance

© Baedeker

Car Park

1 El Patio del Loro
  (restaurant)
2 Parrot show
  Cafeteria
3 Photographers
4 Toilets

5 Souvenir shop
6 Flamingo Pool
7 Humming-birds
8 Chimpanzee enclosure
9 Crowned cranes
10 Banana plantation

11 Free flight show
  Loro-Vision
12 Pelican Pool
13 Galapagos turtles
14 Bananalandia shop
15 Dolphinarium

species which are threatened with extinction, the parrots are kept in pairs in spacious cages. In addition to parrots there are other exotic birds, turtles, chimpanzees and other animals. In the Loro Show parrots of many colours perform their tricks, and there is also a presentation by parrots in free flight. In the Loro-Vision show in the panoramic cinema, with a curved projection area covering 180 degrees, human activities are shown as a bird would see them. The park has been enlarged several times since 1972, the newest attraction being a dolphinarium opened in January 1987.

On entering the park visitors are given a copy of a free guide. Fuller information can be found in a booklet in several languages, with colour illustrations, "Loro Parque Tenerife". (Free bus service from Playa Martiánez/Café Columbus. Buses every 20 minutes; last bus from Loro Parque at 6.45 p.m.)

Puerto de Santiago   C6

Altitude: sea-level
Population: 800

Puerto de Santiago is a small fishing village on the west coast of Tenerife, noted for the formidable cliffs on the coast to the north, the Acantilado de los Gigantes.

Situation and characteristics

It is very evident that this tiny village is a rising tourist resort, for its modest houses are now being surrounded by hotels and bungalows. On the south side of the village is a short sandy beach, the Playa de la Arena.

The village

* Los Gigantes

This holiday development 1 km ($\frac{3}{4}$ mile) north of Puerto de Santiago takes its name from the sheer cliffs, the Acantilado de los Gigantes, which rear up to a height of 500 m (1650 ft) and fall steeply down to the sea just to the north of the settlement. The planning and design of Los Gigantes is of the highest

Loro Parque . . .   *. . . and its parrots*

quality, and – with a single tower block hotel as the exception – the apartment houses and bungalows fit inobtrusively into their setting. There is a boating marina.

This is a place for those who like a quiet holiday, for Los Gigantes is remote from other tourist resorts and offers only a limited range of entertainment. There are no good sandy beaches in the vicinity.

From Los Gigantes there are boat trips along the cliff-fringed coast to the Punta de Teno, the western tip of Tenerife.

Punta del Hidalgo

See Bajamar

Punta de Teno

See Buenavista

San Andrés   A/B10

Altitude: sea-level
Population: 1000

Situation and characteristics

San Andrés is a prosperous fishing village 8 km (5 miles) north-east of Santa Cruz, noted for its modest but good restaurants and for its beach of Las Teresitas.

San Andrés is a good centre from which to explore the Montañas de Anaga (see entry).

The village

San Andrés has managed to preserve much of its original character, having so far remained unspoiled by any large hotel complexes or other tourist facilities. Its Castillo was destroyed some 30 years ago by a storm tide.

Playa de las Teresitas

The Playa de las Teresitas, at the north-east end of San Andrés, is a man-made beach. In the early 1970s the San Andrés Bay was closed off by a breakwater to provide safe bathing and the beach was built up with sand brought direct by boat from the Sahara. Large numbers of palms have been planted to improve the amenity of the beach, which in spite of its nearness to a city is remarkably clean and well maintained. It is frequented mainly by local people.

San Cristóbal de la Laguna

See La Laguna

The resort of Los Gigantes, with the cliffs from which it takes its name

Playa de las Teresitas

San Juan de la Rambla   B8

Altitude: 63 m (207 ft)
Population (district): 4500

Situation and characteristics

San Juan de la Rambla, chief place in the district of that name, lies on the north coast of Tenerife, half-way between Icod and Puerto de la Cruz. As its name indicates (*rambla* = stream, torrent), it lies on a tongue of land formed from deposits carried down by the Barranco Ruiz.

The village

San Juan de la Rambla is a long straggling village, in the centre of which is the simple village church, with a handsome tower.

San Miguel de la Palma

See La Palma

Santa Cruz (Santa Cruz de Tenerife)   B10

Altitude: 0–200 m (0–650 ft)
Population: 210,000

Situation and characteristics

Santa Cruz, capital of the Spanish province of that name and of the island of Tenerife, lies in a sheltered bay at the foot of the Anaga Hills in the north-east of the island. The town owes its economic importance to the steady development of its harbour. Thanks to its situation at the intersection of important Atlantic seaways it is one of Spain's largest ports, handling some 13·6 million tonnes of freight annually. Major contributions are also made to the city's economy by an oil-refinery, chemical manufacturing plants, fish-processing and cigar-making factories.

Visitors are attracted to Santa Cruz by its excellent shopping facilities – by far the best on the island.

History

The history of the town begins in 1492, when Alonso Fernández de Lugo landed in the uninhabited bay which was later to become the site of Santa Cruz. From here he set out on the conquest of the island, and in 1494 he founded the town. In subsequent centuries Santa Cruz had repeatedly to defend itself against attack. In 1657 Admiral Blake tried unsuccessfully to take the town; in 1706, during the War of the Spanish Succession, an attack by Admiral Jennings was beaten off, and at the end of the same century Nelson himself had no better luck. On 22 July 1797 he appeared off Santa Cruz with eight warships and bombarded the town's defences but was forced to retire under the return bombardment by the defenders, in the course of which he lost his right arm.
Another important date in the town's history was 1723, when Santa Cruz became the administrative centre of the archipelago in place of La Laguna, preserving this status until 1927, when the Canaries were divided into two provinces.

Although the tourist and holiday trade makes a major contribution to the economy of Tenerife, little of this is felt in the island's capital, which has preserved its own distinctive atmosphere.

In recent years numbers of handsome new buildings have been erected in the city centre, and modern office blocks and shops now dominate the Plaza de España and the Calle de Castillo pedestrian zone. Here and round the harbour there is perpetual hectic activity. A quieter part of the city is the area round the Parque Municipal García Sanabria, where the well-to-do citizens of Santa Cruz have their houses. The large numbers of inhabitants who are less well off, however, live in the continually expanding housing areas on the outskirts of the city, which is now gradually joining up with La Laguna.

Plaza de España

The flower-decked Plaza de España, near the harbour, is the hub of the city's life. From the square, which is surrounded by car parks, the main traffic arteries of Santa Cruz radiate.

Monumento de los Caídos

In the centre of the square rises the Monumento de los Caídos, which commemorates the dead of the Spanish Civil War (1936–39). In the base of the monument is a memorial chapel. From the top, reached by lift, there are magnificent views of the city and the harbour but the monument is open only on special occasions.

Plaza de España

Palacio Insular

On the west side of the Plaza de España lies the Palacio Insular, a huge complex housing the island administration (the Cabildo Insular), the National Tourist Office and the Archaeological Museum (see below).

Muelle Sur

To see something of the bustling activity round the harbour it is worth taking a stroll along the Muelle Sur (South Mole), where the large passenger and cargo ships and deep-sea fishing-boats moor.

Plaza de la Candelaria

Adjoining the Plaza de España on the west is the Plaza de la Candelaria, an elongated square (closed to traffic) which is surrounded by banks and offices.

Casino de Tenerife

On the corner of the two squares stands the Casino de Tenerife, the premises of the island's oldest private club. The building dates from the middle of the 18th c. and is decorated with murals by leading Canarian painters (seen only with special permission).

Triunfo de la Candelaria

In the centre of the square is a work in early Neo-classical style by the Italian sculptor Antonio Canova (1757–1822), the "Triunfo de la Candelaria" ("Triumph of the Virgin of Candelaria", 1778), in Carrara marble. The Madonna de la Candelaria, patroness of the Canaries, stands on a slender column with figures of four Guanche chieftains at her feet.

Calle de Castillo

The city's principal shopping street, the busy Calle de Castillo, runs north-west from the Plaza de la Candelaria – crowded, particularly in the late afternoon and early evening, with an apparently endless stream of shoppers, window-shoppers and promenaders.

*Museo Arqueológico

Location:
Avenida Bravo Murillo

Opening times:
daily 9 a.m.–1 p.m. and
4–6 p.m.

The Archaeological Museum, on the second floor of the Palacio Insular, has the largest collection of material on the history and culture of the original inhabitants of the Canaries after the Museo Canario in Las Palmas on Gran Canaria. The exhibits on display include more than 1000 skulls, mummies, implements, sherds of pottery, and simple jewellery and everyday objects of the pre-Hispanic period. There are also weapons dating from the time of the Spanish conquest. One room contains a collection of material from the western Sahara.

Labels and explanations are in Spanish. Sets of slides are on sale at the information desk at the entrance to the museum.

Museo Municipal de Bellas Artes

Location:
Calle José Murphy 4

Opening times:
Tue.–Fri. 2–7 p.m., Sat.
9 a.m.–1 p.m.

The Municipal Museum of Art, opened in 1900, is housed in a former Franciscan friary.
The collection, displayed on two floors, includes many pictures and works of sculpture by contemporary Canarian artists and works by Spanish, Flemish and Italian masters, including

Ribera, Brueghel, Madrazo, Van Loo, Jordaens and Guido Reni.

The museum also contains a number of ship models, a collection of arms and armour and a coin collection. The Municipal Library is in the same building.

The Plaza del Príncipe, in front of the museum, was originally the friary garden.   Plaza del Principe

Iglesia de San Francisco

The Iglesia de San Francisco, adjoining the Museum of Art, was founded in 1680 as the church of the Monastery of San Pedro de Alcántara. Much restored in the 18th c., it has two retablos of the 17th and 18th c. The church has a fine organ, and there are frequent recitals.

*Iglesia de Nuestra Señora de la Concepción

The city's oldest and most important church, the Iglesia de Nuestra Señora de la Concepción, was built in 1502. After being damaged by fire in 1652 it was extensively restored during the 17th and 18th c. Its bell-tower (mid 18th c.) was long regarded as the town's principal landmark and emblem. The church, with a low nave flanked by double aisles, contains fine works of Baroque art, including the High Altar, with a figure of the Mater Dolorosa by Luján Pérez, and the marble and

Iglesia de Nuestra Señora de la Concepción   *Plaza de Weyler*

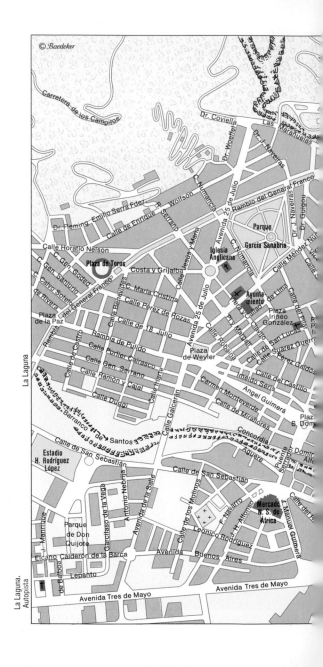

© Baedeker

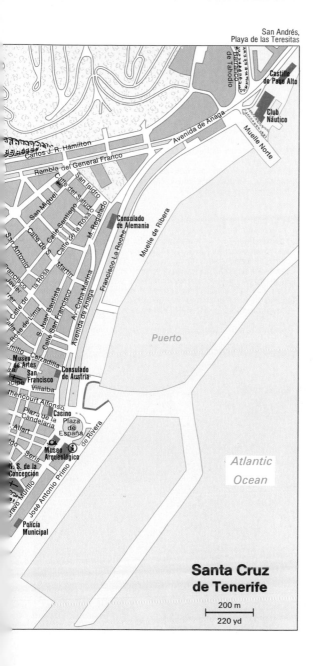

San Andrés,
Playa de las Teresitas

Castillo
de Paso Alto

Club
Náutico

Muelle Norte

Avenida de Anaga

Carlos J. R. Hamilton

Rambla del General Franco

Calle del Saludo

San Isidro

San Miguel

Calle de

Calle Santiago

Calle Ca. la Rosa

M. Regalado

Consulado
de Alemania

Muelle de Ribera

Francisco La Roche

San Antonio

La Rosa

Martín

Francisco
Javier

Calle de
Lima

Av. Cuba Marina

Avenida de Anaga

Calle Juan Bautista

Calle San Francisco

Rosa de Lima

Puerto

Carballo

Museo
de Artes

San
Francisco

Consulado
de Austria

Villalba

Bethencourt Alfonso

Plaza de la
Candelaria

Casino

Plaza
de
España

Callart

Seris

de Rivera

Museo
Arqueológico

N. S. de la
Concepción

Atlantic
Ocean

Bravo Murillo

José Antonio Primo

Policía
Municipal

Santa Cruz
de Tenerife

200 m

220 yd

alabaster pulpit (1736). Also notable are the finely carved choir-stalls. The church also contains various items of historical interest, including such military trophies as the British flags captured during Nelson's unsuccessful attempt to take Santa Cruz.

Castillo de Paso Alto (Museo Militar)

At the north end of the town, just beyond the Club Náutico in the Avenida de Anaga, are the remains of the Castillo de Paso Alto, commonly called the Museo Militar.

On a semicircular outlook platform can be seen five old cannons, including the one known as El Tigre, which took off Nelson's right arm in 1797.

*Parque Municipal García Sanabria

The Municipal Park, one of the largest (6 hectares (15 acres)) and most beautiful in the Canaries, lies to the west of the city centre. Named after a former mayor of Santa Cruz, it contains fine old trees and a profusion of tropical and subtropical plants. Strolling along the shady asphalt paths, visitors inevitably find their way to the huge fountain in the centre of the park. There are also a number of small enclosures for animals, a children's playground and, at the south entrance, a flower clock.

Round the park lies the city's best residential district. In the side

Mercado de Nuestra Señora de África (the principal market of Santa Cruz)

streets are numbers of handsome villas, and the Rambla del General Franco is an imposing wide avenue.

*Mercado de Nuestra Señora de África

From the city centre the Puente Serrador leads to the principal market, in the oldest part of the town. A great round arch gives access to the arcaded central courtyard with its innumerable stalls selling fruit, vegetables, flowers, meat, fish and live animals. Even if they have no intention of buying anything visitors will be fascinated by the Oriental atmosphere of the market.

Near the market, in Calle J. M. Guimerá, are numbers of stalls selling souvenirs, leather goods, domestic equipment and clothing.

Tacoronte   B9

Altitude: 447 m (1467 ft)
Population (district): 16,000

Tacoronte lies 20 km (12½ miles) east of Puerto de la Cruz in a fertile region near the north coast of Tenerife. The town is surrounded by large vineyards – which yield a much-esteemed wine – and arable land. Here agriculture is possible without artificial irrigation. The many caves which have been found in the neighbourhood show that the area was inhabited before the coming of the Spaniards.

Situation and characteristics

Tacoronte is a typical Canarian township, filled with noisy and bustling life in the little side streets. Its two churches are situated below the main street.

The town

The Iglesia de Santa Catalina, built in 1664, has a number of altar-pieces dating from that period and sumptuous silver decoration. The square in front of the church is surrounded by tall Indian laurels.

A few hundred metres away is the other church, the Iglesia del Cristo de los Dolores. This former Augustinian house preserves a much-venerated 17th c. figure of Christ.

Tacoronte, like Icod, also has a fine dragon tree. It stands on the road to Bajamar.

Mesa del Mar

A steep and narrow street flanked by flower-beds descends to the holiday development of Mesa del Mar, 3 km (2 miles) north of Tacoronte. There is a boldly designed hotel complex, and trim bungalows and apartment blocks straggle up the rocky slopes, almost all of them commanding a fine view of the sea. There are a number of small sandy coves for bathing.

*Agua García

2 km (1¼ miles) south of Tacoronte, beyond the Autopista del Norte, lies Agua García, an expanse of dense laurel and heath woodland with the aspect of a primaeval forest.

La Matanza de Acentejo

4 km (2½ miles) south-west of Tacoronte is La Matanza de Acentejo. The name (Massacre of Acentejo) commemorates a bloody encounter in the spring of 1494 between the Guanches and the Spaniards, led by Alonso Fernández de Lugo. After the battle the Spaniards were forced to withdraw to Gran Canaria.

**Teide (Pico de Teide)   C8

Situation and characteristics

The Pico de Teide (3718 m (12,199 ft)), together with the Caldera de las Cañadas (see entry), forms the Parque Nacional del Teide (see entry), which occupies the centre of the island of Tenerife.

Almost everywhere on Tenerife the Pico de Teide dominates the horizon, provided always that it is not shrouded in cloud; and for passengers flying to or from Tenerife or sailing between the islands it long remains a landmark. It is of particularly majestic effect in winter when it is capped with snow. Teide, rearing up 1500 m (4900 ft) above the Caldera de las Cañadas, is the highest peak not only in the Canaries but in the whole of

Teide; in the foreground Los Roques

Spain. In spite of appearances it is not a single regular cone: in fact the real summit, El Pilón (diameter 80 m (88 yd)), rises some 150 m (490 ft) above the Rambleta, an old crater with a diameter of 850 m (930 yd).

The north side of Teide falls steeply down towards the coast. On the south-western and eastern slopes are two outlying spurs, marking old subsidiary craters – to the south-west the Pico Viejo (3135 m (10,286 ft)), and to the east the Montãna Blanca, so called because of its covering of light-coloured lapilli (consisting of phonolites and pumice).

Volcanic activity

The last volcanic eruption in this area occurred in 1798, when for three months lava poured out of vents on the Pico Viejo. The vents are known as Las Narices del Teide (Nostrils of Teide). Teide is now in a solfatara stage, with only residual volcanic activity. Sulphurous vapours at a temperature of 86 °C (189 °F) emanate from the crater and slopes of El Pilón.

Ascent

One of the first ascents of Teide was by Alexander von Humboldt in June 1799. In those days the ascent involved a strenuous climb from the Orotava Valley; nowadays it is possible to enjoy the spectacular view from the summit without undue exertion.

There are four good roads leading to the cableway station at the foot of Teide, providing rapid access from all parts of the island. When wind conditions permit (as is not often the case in winter) the cableway runs daily from the early morning to four o'clock in the afternoon. It takes some 8 minutes to reach the Rambleta (3555 m (11,664 ft)), from which it is a 25 minutes' climb to the summit.

It is also possible even for those without mountaineering experience to ascend Teide on foot from the Montaña Blanca, where a large plan is displayed indicating the route to the summit. In summer the climb can be done in a single day,

Summit of Teide

but it is worth taking two days, spending a night in the *
Altavista Hut, for the sake of seeing the magnificent sunset and
sunrise.

Teno Hills   B/C6/7

Situation

The Teno Hills, immediately west of Teide, occupy the north-
western corner of Tenerife. They are most easily reached from
Buenavista (see entry) or Santiago del Teide.

Topography

The Teno Hills, like the Anaga Hills (see Las Montañas de
Anaga), are formed by old basaltic rocks and look rugged and
inaccessible. Until quite recently the remote villages on the
range could be reached only on narrow hill tracks. The hills rise
to about 1000 m (3300 ft) and fall steeply down to the north
coast.

Santiago del Teide

Santiago del Teide is a popular starting-point for walks and
drives into the hills. The village church is unusual, with white
domes which give it the air of a mosque; it contains a 15th c.
figure of Christ.

**Masca

The most visited place in the Teno range is the hill village of
Masca, to which tours are run by the large travel agencies. It can
be reached in the course of a walk or by car on the narrow road
from Santiago del Teide, or from Buenavista by way of El
Palmar and Las Portelas.

Until the early 1960s Masca was accessible only on mule-
tracks. This remote village is now in contact with civilization
and has been equipped with electric power.

Masca lies at the foot of sheer rock walls, its houses,
surrounded by terraced fields, reaching into a number of small
side valleys. With a plentiful water-supply, the countryside is
green and gay with flowers. The houses are unusual, built on
two levels against the slope of the hill, with a wooden flight of
steps leading up to the entrance. Some of the houses are
abandoned, the inhabitants having left for the towns or
emigrated to other countries to seek a better living.

Walking in the Teno Hills

Apart from the much-visited village of Masca the Teno Hills are
a region almost untouched by tourism. Many of the roads are
bad or not signposted, and it is essential, therefore, to have a
good map.

Barranco de Masca

The Barranco de Masca is one of the most attractive and
botanically one of the most interesting places in the Teno Hills.
It should be explored, however, only with a good local guide.

The walk through the Barranco del Natero is less formidable. From Santiago del Teide the route crosses the Degollada de Cherfe (the pass between Santiago del Teide and Masca) and then by way of the hamlet of Casas de Araza into the gorge. The distance there and back is about 13 km (8 miles).

Santiago del Teide–Barranco del Natero–Santiago del Teide

Erjos lies on the road between Garachico and Santiago del Teide. At first the route passes through a beautiful forest of laurels. Thereafter the vegetation becomes sparser, and the track then descends through terraced fields to El Palmar. It is not necessary to follow the motor road to Buenavista, since there is also a narrow stony footpath. Distance about 17 km (10½ miles).

Erjos–El Palmar–Buenavista

**Valle de la Orotava   B/C8/9

The Valle de la Orotava (Orotava Valley) lies above Puerto de la Cruz in the north of Tenerife. Measuring 10 by 11 km (6 by 7 miles), it is more like a large and gently rising plateau than a valley. In the centre of the valley is the town of La Orotava (see entry).

Situation

The Orotava Valley became famous through Alexander von Humboldt's account of his travels. The landscape of the valley, however, is now very different from what it was in Humboldt's time. The lower parts of the valley have developed into a densely populated area, with older settlements and new developments jostling one another – a sea of houses

Topography

View of the Orotava Valley from La Orotava

interrupted here and there by banana plantations. At heights above 400 m (1300 ft) the bananas give place to fields in which vines, vegetables, fruit and potatoes are grown, with flowering plants providing a colourful setting all the year round. In winter, when the deciduous trees have lost their leaves, the landscape is rather barer, though the tall bushy poinsettias help to make good the deficiency.

This intensively cultivated agricultural region is bounded by a dense belt of forest, with Canary pines and tree heaths flourishing up to 2000 m (6500 ft). Above this begins the barren landscape of the Caldera de las Cañadas (see entry).

Walking in the Valle de la Orotava

The Orotava Valley is good walking country, easily accessible and offering great variety of scenery. There are many organized

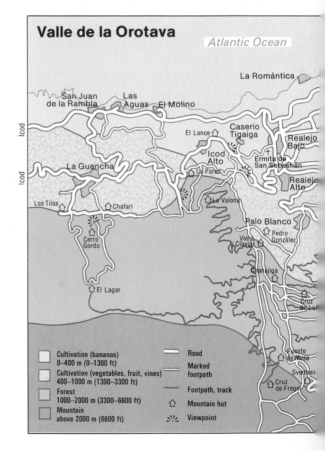

footpaths, mostly well waymarked, and rest and refreshment is available at viewpoints, picnic spots, restaurants and mountain huts. Many of the starting-points of walks can be reached by public transport. See map below.

Vilaflor

D8

Altitude: 1161 m (3809 ft)
Population: 1600

Vilaflor lies 7 km (4½ miles) north-west of Granadilla de Abona on the road which runs from the south of Tenerife to the Caldera de las Cañadas. The highest village in the Canaries, it is surrounded on the north by fragrant pine woods, on the south by plantations of fruit and vegetables. It is famed for its mineral

Situation and characteristics

143

spring, for its pillow lace, and for the wine produced in the surrounding area. Most visitors come to Vilaflor, however, because it is an excellent base for walks and climbs in the Caldera de las Cañadas (see entry).

*The village

Vilaflor is an attractive little village with its little white houses and its many gardens. Narrow streets lead to a square in the upper part of the village, with the Iglesia de San Pedro, which has a 16th c. alabaster statue of St Peter. At the north end of the village are the ruins of an old monastery.

Corpus Christi Procession

The Corpus Christi Procession in Vilaflor takes an unusual form. While in most other places the procession passes over a carpet of flowers, in Vilaflor the carpet is made of volcanic earth. Religious subjects are marked out on the streets with chalk and filled in with volcanic earths of different colours brought from Las Cañadas for the purpose, producing real works of art in an unusual medium.

Practical Information

It is not always possible to give addresses and/or telephone numbers for all places listed in the Practical Information section of these guides. This information is readily obtainable from hotel reception desks or from the local tourist office.

Airlines

Iberia,
Avenida de Anaga 23,
Santa Cruz;
tel. 28 11 00

On Tenerife

Iberia,
Avenida Generalísimo,
Puerto de la Cruz;
tel. 38 00 00

Iberia,
Calle Doctor Quintero 5,
Valverde;
tel. 55 02 78

On Hierro

Iberia,
Calle Apurón 1,
Santa Cruz;
tel. 41 41 43

On La Palma

British Airways,
Calle Gordillo 13 (1st floor),
Las Palmas;
tel. 26 15 86

On Gran Canaria

Air services

Tenerife has two airports. Almost all international flights use the Reina Sofia Airport (Aeropuerto del Sur Reina Sofia), 62 km (39 miles) south-west of Santa Cruz near El Médano. Spanish domestic and particularly inter-island flights mostly use the Los Rodeos Airport (Aeropuerto del Norte Los Rodeos), 13 km (8 miles) north-west of Santa Cruz.

Airports

La Palma's airport, the Aeropuerto Nacional de la Palma, is 8 km (5 miles) south of Santa Cruz.

Hierro's airport, the Aeropuerto Nacional de Hierro, is 7 km (4½ miles) east of Valverde.

Gomera has no airport. It now seems likely, however, that the long-discussed and controversial plan to construct an airport at La Lomada in the commune of Alajeró may be realized in the near future.

From Los Rodeos Airport on Tenerife there are several flights

Inter-island flights

145

Reina Sofia Airport, Tenerife

Hierro Airport can handle only the smaller types of aircraft

daily to La Palma and Hierro and to Gran Canaria and Lanzarote in the eastern Canaries. There is also a daily flight to Fuerteventura.

From La Palma Airport there are several flights daily to Tenerife and Gran Canaria. There are services to Hierro only during the summer months.

From Hierro there are at least two flights daily to Tenerife; services to La Palma only in summer.

Flying times between the islands range between 30 and 50 minutes. Since fares are relatively low, air travel is a popular means of transport with the islanders. Seats should, therefore, be booked in plenty of time, particularly on public holidays and on flights to the smaller islands.

Excess baggage is sometimes carried free or at a small extra charge.

Banks

See Currency

Beaches

The western Canary islands have only relatively short stretches of beach. Gomera, Hierro and La Palma, with only a few coves of grey or black lava sand, are not to be recommended for holiday-makers whose main interest is in bathing. Tenerife has a number of beaches of light-coloured sand (sometimes artificially built up), mainly in the south of the island.

The best beaches on the various islands are listed below.

Beaches on Tenerife

The longest and finest sandy beach on Tenerife extends to the west of the little fishing port and tourist resort of El Médano, in the south of the island. Here, except at the height of the season, it is still possible to find a relatively secluded spot. The only disadvantage is the strong wind which – to the delight of wind-surfers if not of bathers – frequently blows here, carrying blown sand with it.

El Médano

This fishing village, 20 km (12½ miles) west of El Médano, has a sandy beach 400 m (440 yd) long and up to 100 m (110 yd) wide which offers safe bathing even for children. Beach mattresses, sun umbrellas and pedalos can be hired.

Los Cristianos

This artificially built up beach of light-coloured sand, 500 m (550 yd) long by up to 100 m (110 yd) wide, is 3 km (2 miles) north of Tacoronte. A tunnel leads to another cove enclosed by sheer cliffs.

Mesa del Mar

Playa de las Américas, the largest tourist centre in the south of the island, has only three sandy beaches, each 100 m (110 yd) long, separated from one another by rocky reefs. It is advisable, therefore, particularly during the winter season, to book your

Playa de las Américas

147

beach mattress or to occupy a good place on the beach as early in the day as possible. A new beach (Las Vistas) is at present under construction between Playa de las Américas and Los Cristianos.

The two small stretches of beach at the east and west ends of this large tourist centre in the north of the island are not particularly inviting, and the surf on this rocky coast can sometimes be hazardous. The best place for bathers, therefore, is the Lido San Telmo (designed by César Manrique) with its large seawater swimming-pool.

Puerto de la Cruz

This little resort in the west of the island has two small bays of black sand, one immediately below the cliffs of Los Gigantes, the other (Playa de las Arenas) to the south of the village.

Puerto de Santiago

The fishing village of San Marcos, 3 km (2 miles) north of Icod, has a beach of black sand fringed by rugged rocks. Usually not overcrowded, it is frequented both by local people and by visitors. There are a number of pleasant little restaurants along the beach.

San Marcos

The beach of Las Teresitas at San Andrés, 9 km (5½ miles) north-east of Santa Cruz, was built up with sand brought from the Sahara and is protected from the heavy surf by artificial barriers. Since it is mainly frequented by local people, it is usually busy only at week-ends. For a beach so near the city it is extraordinarily clean, and its fringe of palms is an additional attraction.

San Andrés/Las Teresitas

Beaches on Gomera

Playa de Santiago, in the south of the island, has a beach of black sand. There are sometimes dangerous currents here.

Playa de Santiago

The beach by the harbour is uninviting, and bathers should, therefore, make for the Playa de Avalo, 5 km (3 miles) north, with a narrow beach of pebbles and sand 100 m (110 yd) long. It is much frequented by local people at week-ends.

San Sebastián

There are a number of beaches on the Valle Gran Rey coast, in the west of Gomera. The best bathing is on the Playa del Inglés to the north, the Playa Calera to the south and the Playa de las Arenas (two sheltered coves).

Valle Gran Rey

Beaches on Hierro

Most of Hierro's beaches are difficult of access. It is relatively easily to reach the (not particularly inviting) beach of black shingle by the Parador Nacional and the small bay at Tamaduste, 10 km (6 miles) north-east of Valverde. There is also bathing at La Restinga, in the extreme south of the island. In the bay of El Golfo at Los Llanillos is the Charco Azul (Blue Pool), a natural swimming-pool sheltered by a reef which is reached on a stony path. To reach the secluded and attractive beach of El Verodal, at Pozo de la Salud in the north-west of Hierro, a long walk is involved.

◄ *El Médano – a wind-surfer's paradise*

The beach at Los Cristianos, Tenerife

The beach at Puerto Naos, La Palma

Beaches on La Palma

Puerto de Naos owes its modest development as a tourist centre to its 500 m (550 yd) long beach of fine black sand, the best on the island. Sun umbrellas for hire; showers. To the south is the beach of Charco Verde.

Puerto de Naos

The beach of Puerto de Tazacorte (lava sand and pebbles) with its fishing boats is picturesque but not particularly suitable for bathing.

Puerto de Tazacorte

Some 5 km (3 miles) south of the island's capital is the Playa de los Concajos. Some coves here have a narrow sandy beach; others are rocky. Bizarrely shaped reefs serve as breakwaters, making the bathing usually safe.

Santa Cruz

Naturist bathing beaches

On Tenerife the most popular beach for nude bathing is the one at El Médano. At most of the island's tourist resorts topless bathing is acceptable.
On Gomera nude bathing is common on the beaches of Valle Gran Rey.
Hierro and La Palma, on the other hand, are relatively untouched by tourism, and nude bathing tends to raise eyebrows. La Palma has, however, one official naturist beach at Charco Verde (Las Monjas).

Boat trips

See Excursions

Bookshops

Newspaper kiosks and supermarkets offer a limited choice of light literature, much of it in English. The following is a selection of bookshops with a rather wider range of foreign literature.

Tenerife

La Isla Libros,
Calle Robayna 2,
Santa Cruz

Librería Bárbara,
Calle Juan Pablos Abril 36,
Los Cristianos
(closed Wednesday and Saturday afternoon)

Librería De Frank,
Rambla de Pulido 43,
Santa Cruz

Librería Goya,
Calle Pérez Galdós 4,
Santa Cruz

Librería Tenifer,
Calle Delgado Barreto 36,
La Laguna
(opposite the University)

Gomera   Librería Domínguez,
                          La Hurona,
                          Valle Gran Rey

Hierro, La Palma   Visitors to Hierro and La Palma should take sufficient reading
                          material with them, since they will find only a very limited
                          choice on these islands.

Bus services

See Transport

Camping

Camp sites   Camping Sanssouci,
                          Adeje,
                          Tenerife;
                          tel. 78 03 34

                          Camping Nauta,
                          Cañada Blanca,
                          Arona,
                          Tenerife;
                          tel. 78 51 18

                          There are no official camping sites on Gomera, Hierro or La
                          Palma. On La Palma camping is permitted on a specially marked
                          site in the Caldera de Taburiente.

"Camping sauvage"   "Wild" camping is permitted in many places. Before camping
                          in a nature park, however, permission must be obtained from
                          ICONA, Avenida de Anaga 35, Santa Cruz de Tenerife (tel.
                          28 64 00). In Spain it is normally permitted to spend one night
                          on the same spot in a trailer or motor caravan.

Car rental

Tenerife   Avis,
                          Calle Imeldo Seris 21,
                          Santa Cruz;
                          tel. 24 12 94–95
                          and
                          Avenida Venezuela,
                          Puerto de la Cruz;
                          tel. 38 45 52

                          (Also at both airports and at Playa de las Américas and Costa
                          del Silencio)

Hertz,
Avenida de Anaga 7,
Santa Cruz;
tel. 27 48 05
and
Calle de Agustín de Béthencourt,
Puerto de la Cruz;
tel. 38 47 19

(Also at Reina Sofia Airport and San Isidro)

InterRent,
Terminal de Autobuses,
Santa Cruz;
tel. 38 18 00
and
Avenida del Generalísimo 25,
Puerto de la Cruz;
tel. 38 40 52

(Also at both airports and Playa de las Américas)

Avis,   Gomera
Caseta del Muelle 21,
San Sebastián;
tel. 87 04 61

Autos Piñero,
Calle del Medio 147,
San Sebastián;
tel. 87 00 55
and
Carretera General Vuelta el Puerto,
Valle Gran Rey;
tel. 80 53 97

Auto Cruz Alta,   Hierro
Aeropuerto Nacional de Hierro;
tel. 55 00 04
and
La Caleta;
tel. 55 01 16

Avis,   La Palma
Calle O'Daly 32,
Santa Cruz;
tel. 41 14 80

Rent a Car,
Avenida Marítima 69,
Santa Cruz;
tel. 41 24 49

For a car in the lowest category the international car rental firms   Rates
charge between 3000 and 4000 pesetas a day according to the
period of hire. The rates cover unlimited mileage (except on
Hierro).

Comprehensive insurance costs about 600 pesetas a day.
These rates are often undercut by the smaller hire firms.

Practical Information

Chemists

Chemists' shops are open Monday to Friday 9 a.m.–1 p.m. and 4–8 p.m., Saturday 9 a.m.–1 p.m. At other times there is always a "duty pharmacy" open in places of any size. The address is given in a notice headed "Farmacía de Guardia" in every chemist's window. After 10 p.m. only medicines on prescription are issued.

Church services

Protestant

Puerto de la Cruz: every Sunday at 5 p.m. in the Anglican church in the Parque Taoro.

Santa Cruz: first Sunday in the month at 10 a.m. in the church in the Plaza de los Patos.

Los Cristianos: second and fourth Sundays in the month at 11 a.m. in the Casa Sueca.

Playa de las Américas: first and third Sundays in the month at 11.30 a.m. in the Pueblo Canario.

Roman Catholic

Puerto de la Cruz: Wednesday and Saturday at 6.30 p.m. and Sunday at 9.30 and 11 a.m. in the Chapel at San Telmo.

Cinemas (Movie Theatres)

Most cinemas show only films which have been dubbed into Spanish, but some hotels can offer video films in English.

Consulates

United Kingdom

Calle de Suárez Guerra 40 (5th floor),
Santa Cruz de Tenerife;
tel. 24 20 00

Edificio Cataluña,
Calle de Luis Morote 6 (3rd floor),
Las Palmas de Gran Canaria;
tel. 26 25 08

United States

Calle Franchy Roca 5,
Las Palmas de Gran Canaria;
tel. 27 12 59

Currency

The unit of currency is the Spanish peseta (pta). There are banknotes for 200, 500, 1000, 2000, 5000 and 10,000 pesetas and coins in denominations of 1, 5, 10, 25, 50, 100 and 200 pesetas.

100 pesetas=£0·49 sterling	£1 × 205 pesetas	Exchange rates
100 pesetas=US $0.80	$1 =125 pesetas	(subject to fluctuation)

Visitors to Spain may take in up to 150,000 pesetas per head, and may take out a maximum of 100,000 pesetas.
There are no restrictions on the import of foreign currency, but to avoid any difficulties on leaving the country it is advisable to declare any large sums brought in (over the equivalent of 100,000 pesetas).
Foreign currency may be exported up to the equivalent of 500,000 pesetas or a larger amount if declared on entry.
It is advisable to take travellers' cheques or Eurocheques rather than large amounts of cash.

Currency regulations

Account-holders of the British National Girobank, with Postcheques and a special card, can draw the equivalent of £65 at a time from Spanish post offices.

Girobank

The large hotels and better-class restaurants, car hire firms, airlines and shops usually accept the major charge and credit cards (American Express, Diners Club, Access, Eurocard, Visa, etc.).

Credit cards

Money can be changed at banks (open Monday to Friday 9 a.m.–2 p.m., Saturday 9 a.m.–1 p.m.), exchange offices, travel agencies and the reception desk in the larger hotels. It is always changed at the official rate, but commission charges may vary considerably.

Changing money

Customs regulations

The following items may be taken into Spain without payment of duty: clothing for visitors' personal use, toilet articles and other everyday requirements (including cameras and camping gear), and small quantities of food for the journey. For articles of some value, such as portable radios, television sets and video apparatus, visitors may be asked to make a deposit equivalent to the value of the articles.

Entry

Personal effects, etc., may be taken out without formality.

Exit

Doctors

See Medical care

Drinks

See Food and drink

Electricity

Normally 220 volts. In the large hotels the power sockets take plugs of normal European type (with prongs which are thinner and set slightly farther apart than in the British type). Appliances with plugs of non-European type will require adaptors. Outside the large hotels there may often be sockets of a different type, for which adaptors can be bought locally.

Emergency calls

Fire service (Bomberos)	Tenerife: Santa Cruz, tel. 22 00 80; Puerto de la Cruz, tel. 33 00 80 La Palma: tel. 41 11 50
Police (Policía)	Tenerife: tel. 091 La Palma: tel. 41 40 43
Municipal police (Policía municipal)	Tenerife: Santa Cruz, tel. 092; Puerto de la Cruz, tel. 38 04 28 Gomera: tel. 87 00 62 Hierro: tel. 55 00 25 La Palma: tel. 41 11 50
Red Cross (Cruz Roja)	Emergencies on all islands: tel. 28 29 24 Ambulance transport on all islands: tel. 28 18 00
Casualty stations (Casas de socorro)	Tenerife: Santa Cruz, tel. 24 15 02; Puerto de la Cruz, tel. 38 38 12 Gomera: tel. 87 10 51 Hierro: tel. 55 00 79 La Palma: tel. 41 21 40
Hospitals	See Medical care

Events

In this section we list only the most important events and those most likely to be of interest to visitors.

Patronal festivals (the feasts of the local patron saints) usually involve not only a pilgrimage but a variety of secular celebrations and entertainments – Canarian wrestling (*lucha canaria*), a fair, musical performances, boat trips, etc.

5 January	Santa Cruz/Tenerife: Cabalgada de los Reyes Magos. The coming of the Three Kings is celebrated with a colourful procession in the harbour.
6 January	Garachico/Tenerife and Valle Gran Rey/Gomera: Los Reyes, the feast of the Three Kings.
17 January	Fuencaliente/La Palma: patronal festival of San Antonio Abad.
20 January	San Sebastián/Gomera: patronal festival of San Sebastián.
22 January	Los Realejos and Garachico/Tenerife: patronal festival of San Sebastián.
	Icod/Tenerife: patronal festival of San Antonio Abad.

Santa Cruz/Tenerife: Festival of Classical Music; performances in Teatro Guimerá.

January/February

Many places: Carnival.

February

The Carnival is celebrated with the most lavish splendour in Santa Cruz/Tenerife. The "official" programme begins fully two weeks before Ash Wednesday with the choice of the Carnival Queen, and during the following days and weeks there is a succession of musical performances, dancing displays and colourful processions. The high spot of the Carnival is Shrove Tuesday, when all the "registered" groups parade along the Avenida de Anaga. But the celebrations are by no means over on Ash Wednesday.

The "Burial of the Sardine" is a great annual spectacle, when thousands of people assemble outside the bullring to pay the last honours to their sardine, whose ceremonial cremation in the Plaza de España is followed by a gay street festival.

Candelaria/Tenerife: Feast of Nuestra Señora de la Candelaria.

2 February

Mazo/La Palma: patronal festival of San Blás.

3 February

Güimar/Tenerife: village festival in Barrio del Socorro.

7 February

La Laguna/Tenerife: patronal festival of San Benito Abad.

2 March

Garafía/La Palma: patronal festival of San Vicente.

5 March

La Guancha, Tanque/Tenerife and Breña Baja, Fuencaliente/La Palma: patronal festival of San José.

19 March

Many places: Semana Santa (Holy Week), with many processions and other religious and secular celebrations.

March/April

Santa Cruz/Tenerife: Spanish Festival; theatrical and ballet performances.

April

Icod, Tegueste/Tenerife and Agulo/Gomera: patronal festival of San Marcos.

25 April

Santa Cruz/Tenerife: Fiestas de Primavera (Spring Festival); operatic and folk performances, fireworks.

May

Santa Cruz/Tenerife: celebrations commemorating the foundation of the city.

1–5 May

Araya, Granadilla, Los Realejos/Tenerife: patronal festival of San Isidro.

15 May

Many places: Corpus Christi; processions passing over magnificent carpets of flowers and volcanic earth (particularly impressive on Tenerife, at La Orotava and Vilaflor).

June

Many places of La Palma: Fiesta de la Virgen de las Nieves (Festival of Our Lady of the Snows), celebrated every 5 years (1990, 1995, etc.). The celebrations last several weeks; the high spot is the Bajada (Descent) de la Virgen de las Nieves, when the statue of the island's patroness is carried to Santa Cruz in a nocturnal procession.

June (every 5 years)

14 June	Granadilla/Tenerife: patronal festival of San Antonio de Padua.
24 June	Arico, Icod/Tenerife: patronal festival of San Juan.
29 June	Güimar/Tenerife: Fiestas de San Pedro.
First Sunday in July (every 4 years)	Many places on Hierro: Bajada de la Virgin de los Reyes, celebrated every 4 years (1989, 1993, etc.), when the statue of the island's patroness is carried from the Santuario de Nuestra Señora de los Reyes to Valverde. In the following 4 weeks there are numerous musical, dancing and wrestling events.
First Sunday in July	La Laguna/Tenerife: Fiesta y Romería de San Benito Abad; pilgrimage, with popular fiesta.
15 July	Puerto de la Cruz/Tenerife: Fiestas del Gran Poder de Dios; fiesta, with fireworks, exhibitions and other events.
16 July	Santa Cruz/Tenerife: Fiesta de Nuestra Señora del Carmen; popular fiesta.
25 July	Santa Cruz/Tenerife: celebrations commemorating the defence of the town against Nelson in 1797.
5 August	Santa Cruz/La Palma: Fiesta de Nuestra Señora de las Nieves, honouring the island's patroness.
14–15 August	Candelaria/Tenerife: Romería de la Virgen de la Candelaria. This is the greatest festival in the Canaries, which honours the patroness of the archipelago and which draws tens of thousands of people every year.
16 August	Garachico/Tenerife: Romería de San Roque (pilgrimage).
Last Sunday in August	El Cedro, Hermigua/Gomera: Fiesta del Cedro, honouring Nuestra Señora de Lourdes.
30 August	Los Cristianos/Tenerife: patronal festival of Nuestra Señora del Carmen.
About 6 September	San Sebastián/Gomera: fiesta commemorating Columbus's departure for the New World.
7–15 September	La Laguna/Tenerife: Fiestas del Santísimo Cristo.
Sunday following 17 September	Icod/Tenerife: Fiestas del Cristo del Calvario.
3 October	Fasnia/Tenerife: patronal festival of Nuestra Señora del Rosario.
	San Sebastián/Gomera: patronal festival of Nuestra Señora de Guadalupe.
10 October	Valverde/Hierro: patronal festival of the Virgen del Rosario.
21 October	Adeje/Tenerife: patronal festival of Santa Úrsula.
16 November	Guía de Isora/Tenerife: Fiestas del Volcán (popular fiesta).
November/December	Santa Cruz/Tenerife: operatic performances.

Many places, particularly in Santa Cruz/Tenerife: Fiestas de Navidad; a varied programme of pre-Christmas and Christmas celebrations, with exhibitions and other events.

December

Excursions

Holiday-makers in the main tourist centres on Tenerife are offered an inexhaustible range of coach trips by local agencies. Among the most popular excursions are a tour of the island, shorter trips to Las Cañadas, the Anaga Hills and the Teno Hills, and shopping trips to Santa Cruz and Puerto de la Cruz.

By coach

The other islands in the western Canaries have much less to offer. On Gomera and La Palma there are circular tours of the islands, but on Hierro visitors must make their own arrangements for sightseeing.

There is no difficulty about touring any of the islands with a rented car (see Car rental, Suggested itineraries).

By car

A wide variety of boat trips are on offer, ranging from short trips along the coast or day trips to cruises lasting several days. Particularly popular are excursions to Gran Canaria and Lanzarote ($2\frac{1}{4}$ days). For variety of scenery a day trip from Tenerife or Gomera (or vice versa) is to be recommended.

By boat

Visitors can make their own arrangements for sightseeing, but on Gomera it is essential to rent a car: the island's capital has little to offer. Another rewarding day excursion is a trip on the jetfoil which plies between Santa Cruz (Tenerife) and Las Palmas (Gran Canaria), taking only 80 minutes for the crossing. Day trips to the other islands are not worth while in view of the greater distances involved.

Since each of the Canary Islands has its own distinctive character and air fares are relatively low (see Air services), a day trip by air to one of the other islands offers variety of scenery and interest at very reasonable cost. Combined air and coach tours can be booked through travel agencies.

By air

Also on offer are short trips by air to Dakar in Senegal and Marrakesh in Morocco.

Food and drink

A light breakfast (*desayuno*) is followed by a substantial lunch (*almuerzo*) and dinner (*cena*). The two main meals are usually of three courses.

Meals and meal-times

The Canarians usually have lunch between 1 and 3.30 p.m., dinner between 8 and 10.30 p.m. The large hotels and restaurants, however, now often serve meals at the rather earlier times to which most visitors are accustomed.

Elaborately prepared dishes are not to be looked for in the cuisine of the Canaries, but visitors will be surprised to discover

Canarian cuisine

how good the local seafood or the substantial meat dishes can be. As in mainland Spain, much use is made of olive oil, garlic and a variety of herbs.

Restaurants and hotels tend to offer an international cuisine, usually of no more than standard quality. In the smaller places and in country restaurants it is well worth trying some of the local dishes.

Tapas

For a snack between meals or as a preliminary to a meal there are the inevitable *tapas* (appetisers). Bars and bodegas as well as restaurants offer a selection of these tasty titbits, which may include goat's-milk cheese (*queso blanco*), olives, smoked ham (*jamón*), small pieces of fried fish and other seafood.

Gofio

Gofio, made from roasted wheat, maize or barley flour, was the staple food of the original population of the Canaries and is still an essential element in the diet of the islanders, though it is unlikely to appear on a restaurant menu. It is eaten with various dishes in place of bread, and can be either sweet or salt.

Soups

Visitors staying in coastal resorts should try the local fish soup (*sopa de pescado*), which at its best will include a variety of different kinds of fish, mussels and other shellfish, together with vegetables. *Escaldón* is a thick soup made with gofio, *potaje de verdura* a substantial vegetable soup.

Fish dishes

Fish (*pescado*) features prominently in the cuisine of the Canaries, usually grilled or fried. *Vieja* is a very tasty fish similar to carp; it may be either fresh or dried. Also popular is *sancocho* (dried fish parboiled with potatoes, onions and garlic). Other fish dishes found almost everywhere are *calamares a la romana* (deep-fried cuttlefish rings) and *gambas a la plancha* (grilled prawns).

Meat dishes

Visitors who prefer meat (*carne*) will find a choice of pork (*cerdo*), mutton (*carnero*), lamb (*cordero*) and rabbit (*conejo*), which may be either grilled or roasted. There are also typical meat dishes with unusual combinations of ingredients; among them is *puchero*, a stew of different kinds of meat and vegetables, varying according to season.

Mojo

Canarian fish and meat dishes are given their particular flavour by the piquant sauce called *mojo*, made from local herbs, garlic, vinegar and oil. *Mojo rojo* (red mojo) also includes saffron and red peppers, *mojo verde* (green mojo) parsley and coriander.

Papas arrugadas

An essential feature of the Canarian menu is *papas arrugadas* – jacket potatoes boiled in well-salted water. They are eaten in their jackets, which have a white deposit of salt.

Desserts

The people of the Canaries like sweet things, and desserts are always included in the meal. Very tempting, but with a high calorie content, are *bienmesabe* (whipped almond cream with egg and honey), *turrones* (almond cakes), *flan* (crème caramel), *frangollo* (a sweet made of maize flour and milk) and of course *helados* (ices) and fresh fruit. An attractive speciality in some restaurants is flambé bananas.

Drinks

The local mineral water (*agua mineral*) is excellent; it may be either still (*sin gas*) or carbonated (*con gas*). Beer (*cerveza*) and wine are commonly drunk with meals. The local country wine (*vino del país*), either red or white, is rarely to be had; it is normally mixed with wine from mainland Spain. The Canaries have long been celebrated for their Malvasía (Malmsey) and muscatel wines.

The meal will usually end with coffee, either *café solo* (without milk), *café cortado* (with a little milk) or *café con leche* (white coffee). A further variant is *carajillo* (black coffee with a shot of brandy or rum).

Getting to Tenerife

Most visitors to the Canaries go by air. There are several flights daily by Iberia, the Spanish national airline, from London to the Reina Sofia Airport in the south of Tenerife, usually with an intermediate stop at Madrid. It is also possible to fly from international airports round the world to Madrid and get a connection from there to Tenerife.

By air

From Tenerife (Los Rodeos Airport in the north of the island) Iberia has several flights daily to the islands of Hierro and La Palma (see Air services). There is no airport on Gomera.

There are also numerous charter flights to Tenerife from London and other European cities, usually as part of a package which includes accommodation but leaves visitors free to spend their time as they wish. There are no charter flights to Hierro or La Palma.

There is a weekly car ferry service run by the Spanish shipping line Compañía Trasmediterránea from Genoa via Palma de Mallorca, Málaga and Cádiz to Santa Cruz de Tenerife. The crossing from Genoa to Tenerife takes just under 6 days, from Cádiz to Tenerife just under two days.
For connections to Gomera, Hierro and La Palma (see Transport).

By sea (car ferries)

Agents in the United Kingdom:

Compañía Trasmediterránea

Melia Travel,
12 Dover Street,
London W1X 4NS;
tel. (01) 491 3881

Hospitals

See Medical care

Hotels

Spanish hotels are officially classified according to function and quality into various types: *hoteles* (singular *hotel*;

Hoteles, hostales, pensiones

Parador Nacional, Hierro

accommodation with or without meals, own restaurant); *hoteles-apartamentos* (like *hoteles*, but with flats or chalets); *hostales* (singular *hostal*; more modest establishments, with or without meals); and *pensiones* (singular *pensión*; guest-houses, fewer rooms, full board only).

Hotels, apartment hotels and *hostales* may be described as *residencias* (no restaurant, but usually providing breakfast).

Paradores

These State-run hotels (Paradores nacionales de turismo), situated at places of particular tourist interest, are usually beautifully sited, offer every comfort and amenity and have excellent trained staff.

Categories

Hotels and other types of accommodation are classed in five categories, ranging from luxury hotels (five stars) to the most modest hotels, hostales or pensions (one star).

The following list of hotels is based on this system of classification. It gives the address, telephone number and number of rooms; establishments with swimming-pools are indicated by the letters SP. The list consists mainly of hotels; hostales are included only where there is insufficient hotel accommodation.

Tariffs

Hotel tariffs vary considerably according to season. The rates given in the following table are based on the official Spanish hotel guide, the "Guía de Hoteles" (1987). They are for a double room; the rate for a single room ranges between 60 and 80 per cent of the tariff for a double room.

Category	Double room
★★★★★	11,000–20,000 ptas
★★★★	5000–11,000 ptas
★★★	3000–7000 ptas
★★	2000–4000 ptas
★	1000–3500 ptas

Hotels on Tenerife

★★★★Náutilus, Av. de las Piscinas 2, tel. 54 05 00, 268 rooms, SP   Bajamar
★★★Neptuno, Carretera Punta Hidalgo, tel. 54 04 04, 97 r., SP
★★★Tinguaro, Urbanización Montamar, tel. 54 11 54, 115 r., SP

★★★El Médano, La Playa 2, tel. 70 40 00, 65 r., SP   El Médano
★★★Playa Sur Tenerife, Los Valos, tel. 70 41 50, 70 r.

★Aguere, Obispo Rey Redondo 57, tel. 25 94 90, 32 r.   La Laguna

★★★Tenerife Tour, Av. del Generalísimo 170, tel. 50 02 00, 91 r., SP   Las Caletillas

★★Parador Nacional Las Cañadas del Teide, tel. 33 23 04, 17 r., SP   Las Cañadas

★★★Princesa Dacil, Camino Penetración, tel. 79 08 00, 330 r., SP   Los Cristianos

Atalaya Gran Hotel, Puerto de la Cruz

163

★★Reverón, Av. General Franco 26, tel. 79 06 00, 40 r.
★★Andrea's, Av. Valle Menéndez, tel. 79 00 12, 42 r.

Playa de las Américas

★★★★Bougainville Playa, Urbanización San Eugenio, tel. 79 02 00, 481 r., SP
★★★★Conquistador, Av.. Litoral, tel. 79 23 99, 485 r., SP
★★★★Europe, Av. Litoral, tel. 79 13 08, 244 r., SP
★★★★Gran Tinerfe, tel. 79 12 00, 358 r., SP
★★★★Las Palmeras, Av. Litoral, tel. 79 09 91, 519 r., SP
★★★★Park Hotel Troya, tel. 79 01 00, 318 r., SP
★★★★Tenerife Sol, tel. 79 10 62, 523 r., SP
★★★Flamingo, Urbanización San Eugenio, tel. 79 12 20, r., SP

Puerto de la Cruz

★★★★★Botánico, Calle Richard J. Yeoward, tel. 38 14 00, 282 r., SP
★★★★★San Felipe, Av. de Colón 13, tel. 38 33 11, 260 r., SP
★★★★★Semiramis, Calle Leopoldo Cologán 12, tel. 38 55 51, 275 r., SP
★★★★Atalaya Gran Hotel, Parque Taoro, tel. 38 46 00, 183 r., SP
★★★★El Tope, Calzada de Martiánez 2, tel. 38 50 52, 216 r., SP
★★★★Florida, Av. Blas Pérez González, tel. 38 50 52, 216 r., SP
★★★★Meliá Puerto de la Cruz, Av. Marqués Villanueva del Prado, tel. 38 40 11, 300 r., SP
★★★★Orotava Garden, Av. Aguilar y Quesada, tel. 38 52 11, 241 r., SP
★★★★Valle-Mar, Av. de Colón 2, tel. 38 48 00, 171 r., SP
★★★Casa del Sol, Urbanización San Fernando, tel. 38 07 62, 45 r.
★★★Don Manolito, Lomo de los Guirres 6, tel. 38 50 12, 49 r., SP
★★★Internacional, Carretera de las Arenas 91, tel. 38 51 11, 111 r.
★★★Marquesa, Calle Quintana 11, tel. 38 31 51, 88 r., SP
★★★Monopol, Calle Quintana 15, tel. 38 46 11, 92 r., SP
★★★San Telmo, Calle San Telmo 18, tel. 38 58 53, 91 r., SP
★Maja, Calle Iriarte 9, tel. 38 38 53, 24 r.

Puerto de Santiago

★★★★Los Gigantes-Sol, Acantilado de los Gigantes, tel. 86 71 25, 225 r., SP

Realejo Alto

★★★★Maritim, Calle Burgado 1, tel. 34 20 12, 461 r., SP
★★Reforma, Urbanización Tierra de Oro, tel. 34 10 00, 31 r., SP

Santa Cruz

★★★★★Mencey, Calle José Naveiras 38, tel. 27 67 00, 303 r., SP
★★★Plaza, Plaza de la Candelaria 9, tel. 24 75 87, 64 r.
★★Anaga, Calle Imeldo Seris 19, tel. 24 50 90, 126 r.
★★Taburiente, Calle Doctor Guigou 25, tel. 27 60 00, 90 r.

Hotels on Gomera

San Sebastian

★★★★Parador Nacional de la Gomera, tel. 87 11 00, 20 r., SP
★★Garajonay, Calle Ruiz de Padrón 15, tel. 87 05 50, 31 r.
★Canarias, Calle Ruiz de Padrón 3, tel. 87 03 55, 19 r.

★Colombina, Calle Ruiz de Padrón 81, tel. 87 12 57, 25 r.

★Amaya, El Paso, tel. 80 00 73, 7 r.   Vallehermoso

Hotels on Hierro

★★★Parador Nacional El Hierro, tel. 55 01 01, 47 r., SP   15 km (9 miles) S of Valverde

★★Boomerang, Calle Doctor Gost 1, tel. 55 02 00, 17 r.   Valverde
★Casañas, Calle San Francisco 5, tel. 55 02 54, 11 r.
★Morales, Calle Licenciado Bueno 7, tel. 55 01 62, 14 r.
★Sanflei, Calle Santiago 18, tel. 55 08 57, 13 r.

Hotels on La Palma

★★Nambroque, Calle Monteluján, tel. 48 52 79, 10 r.   El Paso

★Eden, Calle Angel 1, tel. 46 01 04, 15 r   Los Llanos de Aridane

★★★Parador Nacional de Santa Cruz, Av. Marítima 34, tel.   Santa Cruz
41 23 40–41, 32 r.
★★★San Miguel, Av. El Puente 31, tel. 41 12 43, 70 r.
★★Canarias, Calle A. Cabrera Pinto 27, tel. 41 31 82, 14 r.
★Bahía, Plaza de la Luz 26, tel. 41 18 46, 30 r.

Information

Spanish National Tourist Office,   In the United Kingdom
57–58 St James's Street,
London SW1A 1LD;
tel. (01) 499 0901

Spanish National Tourist Office,   In the United States
665 Fifth Avenue,
New York NY 10022;
tel. (212) 759 8822

845 North Michigan Avenue,
Chicago IL 60611;
tel. (312) 944 0215

1 Hallidie Plaza, Suite 801,
San Francisco CA 94102;
tel. (415) 346 8100

Spanish National Tourist Office,   In Canada
60 Bloor Street West,
Toronto, Ontario M4W 3B8;
tel. (416) 961 3131

Oficinas de Turismo   On Tenerife

Palacio Insular,
Plaza de España,
Santa Cruz;
tel. 24 25 93
Open Monday to Friday 8 a.m.–3 p.m.

Plaza de la Iglesia 3,
Puerto de la Cruz;
tel. 38 43 28
Open Monday to Friday 8 a.m.–1 p.m. and 5–7 p.m., Saturday
9.30 a.m.–1 p.m.

Tourist information offices are being established at Las
Galletas, Playa de las Américas and Los Cristianos.
Useful information can also be obtained from the local offices
of the large travel agencies.

On Gomera

There is no official tourist office on Gomera. For information
apply to the Island Council:

Cabildo Insular,
Calle General Franco 20,
San Sebastián;
tel. 87 01 03

On Hierro

There is a small information desk, with irregular opening hours,
in the airport building.

On La Palma

Oficina de Turismo,
Calle O'Daly 6,
Santa Cruz;
tel. 41 21 06
Open Monday to Saturday 8.30 a.m.–1 p.m. and 5–7 p.m.

Tamanca Information Office,
Calle Viconde del Buen Paso 13,
Los Llanos de Aridane;
tel. 46 11 13
Open Monday to Friday 10 a.m.–1 p.m. and 5–7 p.m., Saturday
10 a.m.–1 p.m.

Information in English, German and Spanish; day trips
organized and accommodation arranged (advance bookings
from abroad accepted).

Telephone enquiries

Information and advice can be obtained by telephone (English
spoken):
Tenerife, tel. 37 19 28
La Palma, tel. 41 61 41

Language

In the larger hotels and restaurants on Tenerife the staff
usually speak either English or German. In remoter places,
and particularly on the smaller islands, language may be a
problem. On La Palma and Hierro it is advisable to have at
least a smattering of Spanish.

Everyday expressions

Good morning	¡Buenos días!
Good afternoon!	¡Buenas tardes!
Good evening, good night!	¡Buenas noches!

Goodbye!	¡Adios! ¡Hasta luego!
Yes, no	Sí, no (señor, etc.)
Please!	¡Por favor!
Thank you (very much)!	¡(Muchas) gracias!
Excuse me! (*e.g. for a mistake*)	¡Perdón!
Excuse me! (*e.g. when passing in front of someone*)	¡Con permiso!
Not at all! (You're welcome!)	¡De Nada! ¡No hay de qué!
Do you speak English?	¿Habla Usted inglés?
A little, not much	Un poco, no mucho
I do not understand	No entiendo
What is the Spanish for . . . ?	¿Cómo se dice en español . . . ?
What is the name of this church	¿Cómo se llama esta iglesia?
The Cathedral (of St John)	La catedral (San Juan)
Where is Calle . . . ?	¿Dónde está la calle . . .
the road to . . . ?	el camino para . . . ?
To the right, left	A la derecha, izquierda
Straight ahead	Siempre derecho
Above, up	Arriba
Below, down	Abajo
When is it open (closed)?	¿A qué horas está abierto (cerrado)?
How far?	¿Qué distancia?
Today	Hoy
Yesterday	Ayer
The day before yesterday	Anteayer
Tomorrow	Mañana
Have you any rooms?	¿Hay habitaciones libres?
I should like . . .	Quisiera . . .
A room with private bath	Una habitación con baño
With full board	Con pensión completa
What does it cost?	¿Cuánto vale?
Everything included	Todo incluído
That is too dear	Es demasiado caro
Bill, please! (*to a waiter*)	¡Camarero, la cuenta, por favor!
Where is the lavatory?	¿Dónde está al retrete?
Wake me at six	Llámeme Usted a las seis
Where is there a doctor?	¿Dónde hay un médico?
a dentist?	un dentista?
a chemist?	una farmacia?
Help!	¡Socorro!
I have a pain here	Siento dolores aquí
I am suffering from . . .	Padezco de . . .
I need medicine for . . .	Necesito un medicamento contra . . .
How often must I take it?	¿Cuántas veces tengo que tomar esta medicina?

Days of the week

Sunday	Domingo
Monday	Lunes

167

Tuesday	Martes
Wednesday	Miércoles
Thursday	Jueves
Friday	Viernes
Saturday	Sábada

Numbers

0	cero		22	veintidós
1	uno, una		30	treinta
2	dos		31	treinta y uno
3	tres		40	cuarenta
4	cuatro		50	cincuenta
5	cinco		60	sesenta
6	seis		70	setenta
7	siete		80	ochenta
8	ocho		90	noventa
9	nueve		100	ciento (cien)
10	diez		101	ciento uno
11	once		153	ciento cincuenta y tres
12	doce		200	doscientos
13	trece		300	trescientos
14	catorce		400	cuatrocientos
15	quince		500	quinientos
16	dieciséis		600	seiscientos
17	diecisiete		700	setecientos
18	dieciocho		800	ochocientos
19	diecinueve		900	novecientos
20	veinte		1000	mil
21	veintiuno		1,000,000	un millón

Geographical, etc., terms

Acantilado	Rocky coast
Ayuntamiento	Town hall
Bahía	Bay
Barranco	Gorge
Barrio	District, quarter (of a town)
Bosque	Wood, forest
Calle	Street
Camino	Road, track, path
Capilla	Chapel
Carretera	(Main) road
Cementerio	Cemetery, churchyard
Ciudad	City, town
Claustro	Cloister
Convento	Monastery, convent
Costa	Coast
Cuesta	Slope, hill
Cueva	Cave
Cumbre	Summit
Ermita	Chapel, small church
Faro	Lighthouse
Fuente	Fountain, spring
Iglesia	Church
Jardín	Garden
Llano	Plain
Mar	Sea

Mirador	Viewpoint
Montaña, monte	Mountain, hill
Paisaje	Landscape
Parque	Park
Paseo	Avenue, promenade
Patio	Courtyard
Peña	Crag, cliff
Pico	Peak, summit
Playa	Beach
Plaza	Square
Pueblo	Village
Puente	Bridge
Puerta	Door(way)
Puerto	Port, harbour; pass
Punta	Point, headland
Río	River
Roque	Rock
Sierra	Mountain range
Torre	Tower
Torrente	Mountain stream
Urbanización	Housing development
Valle	Valley

Language courses

London School of English
(Courses in Spanish and English),
Calle Numancia 3,
Santa Cruz;
tel. 28 17 23

On Tenerife

Pueblo Canario, No. 1,
Playa de las Américas;
tel. 79 16 06

Academia Especializada
(Courses in Spanish),
Calle Iriarte 43,
Puerto de la Cruz;
tel. 38 07 79

Spanish lessons can be arranged through the Tamanca
Information Office in Los Llanos de Aridane (see Information).

On La Palma

Marinas

Real Club Náutico de Tenerife,
Avenida Francisco Larroche,
Santa Cruz, Tenerife;
tel. 27 31 17
No moorings; only 60 anchorages

Puerto Pesquero Los Cristianos,
Los Cristianos, Tenerife;
tel. 79 11 02
No moorings; 200 anchorages

Puerto Deportivo Agigansa,
Acantilado de los Gigantes,
Puerto de Santiago, Tenerife;
tel. 86 71 00
370 moorings

Medical care

There are adequate medical services on all the islands. Most of the doctors speak at least one foreign language. In case of emergency apply to one of the hospitals listed below or to a casualty station (see Emergency calls).

Health insurance

British citizens, like nationals of other EEC countries, are entitled to obtain medical care under the Spanish health services on the same basis as Spanish people. This means that they can get free medical and hospital treatment but will be required to pay charges for prescribed medicines or dental treatment.

Before leaving home they should ask their local social security office for a booklet called "Medical costs abroad" (SA 30), which contains an application for form E 111. This is the document which they must present to the local office of the Instituto Nacional de Previsión when seeking treatment (except in case of emergency).

It is nevertheless advisable, even for EEC nationals, to take out some form of temporary health insurance providing complete cover and possibly avoiding bureaucratic delays, and nationals of non-EEC countries should certainly have insurance cover.

Instituto Nacional de Previsión

On Tenerife:
Calle San Agustín 52, La Laguna, tel. 25 00 04
Calle Cologán 4, La Orotava, tel. 33 18 34
Calle Méndez Núñez 14, Santa Cruz, tel. 28 50 01
Also in Icod and Güimar

On Gomera:
Calle Ruiz de Padrón 2, San Sebastián, tel. 87 02 05

On Hierro:
Delegación del Gobierno, Avenida Dacio Darias, Valverde, tel. 55 01 25

On La Palma:
Calle O'Daly 22, Santa Cruz, tel. 41 11 54

Medical centres on Tenerife with 24-hour emergency service

Centro Médico Dr Juan Ruiz García,
Plaza del Charco 6,
Puerto de la Cruz;
tel. 38 11 11

Centro Médico Internacional,
Pueblo Canario,
Playa de las Américas;
tel. 79 17 11

Clínica Bellevue, Urbanización San Fernando (Parque Taoro), Puerto de la Cruz; tel. 38 35 51	Hospitals on Tenerife

Clínica Bellevue,
Urbanización San Fernando
(Parque Taoro),
Puerto de la Cruz;
tel. 38 35 51

Clínica General,
Urbanización Ofra,
La Laguna
(on La Laguna–Santa Cruz motorway);
tel. 64 10 11

Clínica Quibey,
Rambla del General Franco 115,
Santa Cruz;
tel. 27 39 04

Policlínica Tamaragua,
Calle Valois 15,
Puerto de la Cruz;
tel. 38 06 12

Hospital Insular,   Hospital, Gomera
Barrio El Calvario,
San Sebastián;
tel. 87 09 06

Hospital Insular de Nuestra Señora de los Reyes,   Hospital, Hierro
Avenida Valverde,
Valverde;
tel. 55 00 79

Hospital de Nuestra Señora de los Dolores,   Hospital, La Palma
Plaza de Ramón y Cajal,
Santa Cruz;
tel. 41 21 40

See entry   Emergency calls

Motoring

In the Canaries, as in mainland Spain and the rest of continental Europe, traffic travels on the right, with overtaking (passing) on the left.

120 km p.h. (74½ m.p.h.) on motorways.   Speed limits
100 km p.h. (62 m.p.h.) on roads with two or more lanes in each direction.
90 km p.h. (56 m.p.h.) on other roads.
60 km p.h. (37 m.p.h.) in built-up areas.

Seat belts must be worn outside built-up areas. Children under   Seat belts
10 must travel in the rear seats.

On well-lighted streets and roads (except expressways and   Lights
motorways) driving with sidelights is permitted. A careful
watch should be kept for vehicles driving without lights.

Practical Information

Priority

In general, traffic coming from the right has priority, and this applies even to side streets in towns. Exceptions to the rule are indicated by signs.

Overtaking

When overtaking (passing) the left-hand indicator light must be kept on during the whole process and the right-hand one operated when pulling in to the right. Drivers about to overtake, or approaching a bend, must sound their horn during the day and flash their lights at night.

Overtaking is prohibited within 100 m (110 yd) of a blind summit and on roads with a visibility of less than 200 m (220 yd).

Blood alcohol limit

The blood alcohol limit is 0·8 per 1000.

Breakdown assistance

Visitors travelling in a rented car should contact the office of the firm from which they rented it.

If you have a breakdown in your own car help can be obtained from the Policia Municipal (see Police) in towns and from the Guardia Civil de Tráfico in the country.

Accidents

An accident can have very serious consequences for a foreign driver. Whether the accident is his fault or not, his car may be impounded (and may be released only after the completion of any judicial proceedings that follow), and in serious cases the driver may be arrested.

After any accident the Spanish insurance company named on the driver's "green card" must be informed without delay, so that arrangements may be made for any payment required in the way of bail.

The towing of broken-down vehicles by private cars is prohibited.

In the event of an accident involving a hired car the instructions in the hire documents should be followed.

Automobile clubs

Real Automóvil Club de Tenerife,
Avenida Anaga,
Santa Cruz, Tenerife;
tel. 27 00 70

Touring Club de España,
Calle García Morato 14,
Santa Cruz, Tenerife;
tel. 27 51 08

Museums

Tenerife

Casa de Ossuna
See "A to Z", La Laguna

Museo Arqueológico
See "A to Z", Santa Cruz

Museo Municipal de Bellas Artes
See "A to Z", Santa Cruz

Museo Torre del Conde   Gomera
At present closed

Exposición de Fondos Etnográficos y Arqueológicos   Hierro
See "A to Z", Hierro, Valverde

Museo Juan Padrón
See "A to Z", Hierro, Valverde

Museo de Historia Natural y Etnográfico   La Palma
See "A to Z", La Palma, Santa Cruz (Castillo de Santa Catalina)

Museo Naval
See "A to Z", La Palma, Santa Cruz

Newspapers and periodicals

Major British newspapers and periodicals are on sale on
Tenerife the day after publication, as is the "International
Herald Tribune". On the smaller islands it may take longer, and
the choice will be more restricted.

The English-language "Island Gazette", published monthly,
gives local news and information about excursions, restaurants, etc.

Night life

The Casino Taoro is beautifully situated high above Puerto de   Casino
la Cruz in the Parque Taoro.

Opening times:
Summer: Sunday to Friday 9 p.m.–4 a.m., Saturday 9 p.m.–
5 a.m.

Winter: Sunday to Thursday 8 p.m.–3 a.m., Friday 8 p.m.–
4 a.m., Saturday 8 p.m.–5 a.m.

In the large tourist centres on Tenerife, particularly in Puerto de   Discothèques, night clubs
la Cruz, there are large numbers of discothèques and night
clubs which attract an international clientele. There are no
similar establishments on Gomera, Hierro or La Palma.

Opening times

Monday to Friday 9 a.m.–2 p.m., Saturday 9 a.m.–1 p.m.   Banks

Monday to Friday 9 a.m.–1 p.m. and 4–8 p.m., Saturday 9 a.m.–   Chemists
1 p.m.

Practical Information

Churches	Churches are usually open in the morning and late afternoon as well as for services.
Museums	The opening times of museums vary: see entries in the "A to Z" section.
Offices	Monday to Friday 9 a.m.–1 p.m. and 3–7 p.m., Saturday 9 a.m.–1 p.m.
Petrol stations	Most petrol stations close at 8 or 10 p.m. On Sunday *all* petrol stations are closed.
Post offices	Monday to Friday 9 a.m.–2 p.m., Saturday 9 a.m.–1 p.m.
Shops	Most shops are open Monday to Friday 9 a.m.–1 p.m. and 4–8 p.m., Saturday 9 a.m.–1 p.m.; but there are no fixed closing times in Spain, and supermarkets and other shops, particularly in the tourist centres, are often open outside these hours and sometimes on Sundays as well.

Police

Policia (Police)	Tenerife: Avenida Pérez de Armas, Santa Cruz; tel. 091 Calle Santo Domingo, Puerto de la Cruz; tel. 38 12 24 Plaza León Huertas, Icod de los Vinos; tel. 81 00 19 Gomera: tel. 87 00 62 Hierro: tel. 55 00 25 La Palma: tel. 41 11 50
Policia Muncipal (town and traffic police)	See Emergency calls
Guardia Civil (country police, criminal police)	Tenerife: Finca Tío Pino, Santa Cruz; tel. 22 31 00 Polígono San Felipe, Puerto de la Cruz; tel. 38 35 28 Gomera: El Calvario 27, San Sebastián; tel. 87 02 55 Hierro: Avenida Dacio Darias, Valverde; tel. 55 01 05 La Palma: La Portada, Santa Cruz; tel. 41 11 00

Postal and telephone services

A Spanish pillar-box

All letters and postcards from the Canaries go by air. Mail takes at least five days to reach northern Europe.

Postal service

Postage (to Europe):
letters up to 20 grams	48 ptas
up to 50 grams	85 ptas
postcards	40 ptas

Spanish pillar-boxes (post-boxes) are yellow.

Post-boxes

Post and telegraph offices (Correos y Telégrafos) are open Monday to Friday 9 a.m.–2 p.m., Saturday 9 a.m.–1 p.m.
Telephone calls cannot be made from post offices.

Post offices

Telegrams can be sent from post offices or dictated by telephone (dial 22 20 00).

Telegrams

No dialling code is required for calls within the province of Santa Cruz de Tenerife (which includes the islands of Gomera, Hierro and La Palma).

Telephoning

International calls can be made from coin-operated public telephones bearing the word *interurbana* or *internacional*. These take 20, 50 and 100 peseta coins. To make a call, first dial 07; then, when the high-pitched dialling tone is heard, dial the appropriate international code (44 for the United Kingdom, 1 for the United States or Canada), followed by the local dialling code (omitting an initial zero) and the telephone number. A faint dialling tone is heard during dialling. For a call of some length it is preferable to go to one of the public telephone offices (only in the larger towns, and open only at certain times), where payment is made on termination of the call.

Local (within province of Santa Cruz de Tenerife): 003
International: 91 98

Directory enquiries

From the United Kingdom to the western Canaries (province of Santa Cruz de Tenerife): 010 34 22

Dialling codes

From the United States or Canada to the province of Santa Cruz de Tenerife: 011 34 22

From within Spain to the province of Santa Cruz de Tenerife: 9 22

From within Spain to the province of Las Palmas de Gran Canaria: 9 28

From the Canaries to the United Kingdom: 07 44

From the Canaries to the United States or Canada: 07 1

Public holidays

Fixed feasts

1 January	Año Nuevo (New Year's Day)
6 January	Reyes Magos (Epiphany)
2 February	La Candelaria (Candlemas)
19 March	San José (St Joseph's Day)
1 May	Día del Trabajo (Labour Day)
25 July	Santiago (St James's Day)
15 August	Asunción (Assumption)
12 October	Día de la Hispanidad (discovery of America)
1 November	Todos los Santos (All Saints)
8 December	Inmaculada Concepción (Immaculate Conception)
25 December	Navidad (Christmas Day)

Movable feasts

Jueves Santo (Maundy Thursday)
Viernes Santo (Good Friday)
Corpus Christi

Local feasts

See Events

Radio and television

Most TV programmes in the Canaries are relayed from the mainland and are in Spanish. On short wave radio the BBC World Service and the Voice of America can be heard clearly at night and in the early morning. Brief news and music programmes in English are broadcast mornings and evenings from Las Palmas and twice daily from Tenerife.

Restaurants

Restaurants on Tenerife

Bajamar

Casa Pepe, Tejina, tel. 54 09 58

Candelaria

Ainara, Edificio Olympo, tel. 24 71 23
Casa José, Avenida del Generalísimo 3, tel. 50 04 58

El Médano

Angelo's Way, Avenida Amalia 3, tel. 70 43 75

Garachico

Isla Baja, Calle Esteban de Ponte 5, tel. 83 00 08

La Caleta (Adeje)

Cala Marin, tel. 78 02 41

La Laguna

Casa Tomás, Carretera del Portezuelo, tel. 25 05 47

Las Galletas

Jardín Canario, Calle Bélgica 12, tel. 78 52 76

Los Cristianos

*El Sol, Chez Jaques, Calle El Cabezo, tel. 70 05 69
El Rancho de Don Antonio, Calle Juan XXIII, tel. 79 00 92
Flamingo, Avenida Generalísimo Franco 14, tel. 79 05 96
L'Scala, Calle La Paloma 7, tel. 79 10 51
Málaga, Calle Juan Pablos Abril

La Villa Nueva, Calle Princesa Dacil 31, San Vincente, tel. Los Realejos
34 15 58

Bistro, Edificio Viña del Mar, tel. 79 07 18 Playa de las Américas
Borinquén Tropic, Edificio Borinquén, tel. 79 00 08

*Castillo de San Felipe, Avenida Luis Lavaggi, tel. 38 21 13 Puerto de la Cruz
*Magnolia, Carretera del Botánico 5, tel. 38 56 14
Andrea's, Urbanización La Paz, tel. 38 52 09
El Bistro, Edificio Lavaggi, Avendia Generalísimo, tel. 38 05 21
La Papaya, Calle del Lomo 14, tel. 38 28 12
Marina, Calle José Antonio 1, tel. 38 53 11
Méson Monasterio, La Vera Alta, La Montañeta, tel. 34 07 07
Mi Vaca y Yo, Cruz Verde 3, tel. 38 52 47
Patio Canario, Calle del Lomo 8, tel. 38 04 51

Aioli, Acantilado de los Gigantes, tel. 86 77 28 Puerto de Santiago
Asturias, Acantilado de los Gigantes, tel. 86 72 23

La Caseta, tel. 54 00 32 Punta del Hidalgo

*La Riviera, Rambla General Franco 155, tel. 27 58 12 Santa Cruz
El Coto de Antonio, Calle General Goded 13, tel. 27 21 05
La Estancia, Calle Méndez Núñez 110, tel. 27 20 49
La Fragna, Calle General Antequera 17, tel. 27 74 69
La Masía II, Calle Méndez Núñez 61, tel. 28 99 06
La Troya, Calle Méndez Núñez 104, tel. 28 26 11
Martín Fierro, Rambla General Franco 96, tel. 27 69 42

Vista el Valle, Cuesta de la Ville 52, tel. 30 09 71 Santa Úrsula

El Campo, Carretera General del Norte 342, tel. 56 17 61 Tacoronte
Los Arcos, Carretera General 254, tel. 56 09 65

Restaurants on Gomera

Casa del Mar, Calle General Franco 61, tel. 87 12 19 San Sebastián
El Pajar, Calle Ruiz Padrón 44, tel. 87 11 02

Restaurants on La Palma

La Cascada, Carretera de la Cumbre (km 23·5), tel. 48 57 27 El Paso
Las Piedras, Carretera de la Cumbre, tel. 48 52 79

Bodegas Teneguia, Llano de San Antonio Fuencaliente, tel. Fuencaliente
44 40 78

Su Casa, tel. 44 04 04 Mazo

La Fontana, Playa de los Cancajos, tel. 43 42 50 Santa Cruz

Playa Mont, Puerto de Tazacorte, tel. 48 04 43 Tazacorte

Restaurants, like hotels, are required to have a "complaints Complaints
book" (*libro de reclamaciones*), which is inspected by the
authorities. Complaints by dissatisfied clients should be
entered in this book, giving name and home address; entries
may be made in English.

Shopping

Free trade zone

Since 1852 the Canaries have been a free trade (duty-free) zone. This does not necessarily mean that all prices are low, for shops do not always pass on the benefit of the tax exemption to the customer.

Tobacco goods will be found to be considerably cheaper than at home, and the prices of spirits and perfumes are also relatively low. Cameras and other technical equipment, and also furs, can sometimes be found at prices that appear very reasonable; but purchases should be made only in specialized shops and after a careful check on quality.

The best shopping centres on Tenerife are Santa Cruz and Puerto de la Cruz.

Souvenirs

Tenerife is noted for its artistic hem-stitch embroidery (*calados*), in the form of tablecloths, place-mats and articles of clothing. Another fine local product is Vilaflor lace, which resembles Venetian lace. Basketwork made from palm leaves, reeds and osiers is produced on all the islands. The finest ceramics come from Gomera (Chipude) and La Palma (Mazo), hand-modelled without the use of a wheel and decorated with traditional designs. Seeds and seedlings of indigenous plants, or a bunch of strelitzias (sold in flower shops ready packed for the flight home) will provide an attractive reminder of the flora of the Canaries. For those who like to take back an alcoholic souvenir of their visit there are the Malvasía (Malmsey) wine of Hierro and the local banana liqueur.

Sport

Deep-sea fishing

The Canaries are a paradise for deep-sea anglers, with good fishing grounds only 3 km (2 miles) off the coasts.

The necessary permit for deep-sea fishing can be obtained from the Servicio de Pesca, Avenide de Anaga 35, Santa Cruz de Tenerife.

Diving

Poseidon Nemrad Diving School,
Hotel Palmeras,
Playa de las Américas,
Tenerife

Barracuda Diving School,
Hotel Paraíso Floral,
Adeje,
Tenerife

Club de Pesca Neptuno,
Calle Pérez Galdós 19,
Santa Cruz,
Tenerife

Campo de Golf,   Golf
above Tacoronte, near Los Rodeos Airport,
Tenerife; tel. 25 02 30
18 holes; total length 5·2 km ($3\frac{1}{4}$ miles)

Golf del Sur,
near Reina Sofia Airport, Tenerife
27 holes

On some stretches of coast there are fairly strong winds, making   Sailing, wind-surfing
these areas unsuitable for beginners.

Wind-surfers will find ideal conditions at El Médano on
Tenerife, where there is a wind-surfing school. Boards can be
hired on the beaches of El Médano, Los Cristianos, Playa de las
Américas and Las Teresitas (see Beaches).

The shooting season for small game (partridges, wild pigeons,   Shooting (hunting)
rabbits) is from the first Sunday in August to the last Sunday in
December.

Information from the Sociedad de Cazadore, Calle San Agustín
43, La Laguna, tel. 25 80 35.

Most of the large hotels on Tenerife have excellent tennis   Tennis
courts, sometimes equipped with floodlighting. Coaching is
available. Some hotels (e.g. the Flamingo Hotel at Playa de las
Américas) offer all-in tennis holidays.

See entry   Walking

Of particular interest to visitors are the traditional local sports,   Canarian sports
the best known of which is Canarian wrestling (*lucha canaria*).
In almost every place of any size there is a ring on which
contests are held between twelve-man teams of wrestlers.

The *juego del palo*, a contest like singlesticks, with two sticks
instead of one, is also fascinating to watch. Each contestant has
to attack his opponent and ward off his blows, moving his body
as little as possible.

Another Canarian diversion is cock-fighting, which is the
subject of heavy betting.

There are bullfights several times a year in the Santa Cruz   Bullfights
bullring in Rambla del General Franco, which has seating for
7000 spectators.

Taxis

Most taxis have meters. For journeys of some length, however,
there are fixed rates (e.g. from Puerto de la Cruz to La Laguna
about 1000 ptas one way, 2000 ptas there and back). To avoid
any possibility of dispute it is advisable to ask about the fare
before setting out. The current official tariffs can be seen in
tourist information offices (see Information).
Waiting time is charged extra.

Telegraph and telephone services

See Postal and telephone services

Time

In winter the Canaries observe Greenwich Mean Time, one hour earlier than the time in mainland Spain and five hours later than New York Time. From April to September Summer Time is in force, the same as British Summer Time and five hours later than Eastern Daylight Saving Time in New York.

Tipping

In general a service charge is included in bills, but hotel staff, waiters, taxi-drivers, etc., expect an additional tip of 5–10 per cent of the bill.

Transport

Buses

Almost all towns and villages on Tenerife are connected by a network of bus services. Between Puerto de la Cruz, Santa Cruz and Playa de las Américas there is at least an hourly service.

A jetfoil at full speed

In Santa Cruz all buses start from the bus station in the Avenida Tres de Mayo, at the end of the motorway.

The bus station in Puerto de la Cruz is in the Polígono (beyond the old part of the town), near the Post Office.

In Playa de las Américas the buses leave from the Pueblo Canario, opposite the Hotel Gran Tinerfe.

The bus station in Los Cristianos is beside the taxi office (opposite the petrol station), at the entrance to the town.

Most places on Gomera, Hierro and La Palma are also served by buses, but the services are much less frequent. In general buses leave the outlying towns and villages for the island's capital early in the morning, returning in the afternoon.

See entry   Car rental

See entry   Taxis

See entry   Air services

All the islands are connected by regular services run by the   Boat services
Compañia Trasmediterránea and by the Gomera ferry: see map
on inside back cover. There is a jetfoil service between Santa
Cruz and Las Palmas.

Travel documents

Visitors from the United Kingdom, the Commonwealth and the   Personal papers
United States must have a valid passport. No visa is required by
nationals of the United Kingdom, Australia, Canada and New
Zealand for a stay of up to three months, or by United States
nationals for a stay of up to six months, provided in each case
that they are not taking up any paid employment. An extension
of stay can be granted by the police authorities.

A national driving licence is acceptable in Spain, but must be   Car papers
accompanied by an official translation stamped by a Spanish
consulate; it may be easier and cheaper to carry an international
driving permit (which is required in any event for business
trips).

The car registration document must be carried, and the car must
bear an oval nationality plate.

An international insurance certificate (green card) is required,
and also a bail bond (issued by an insurance company with the
green card), since in the event of an accident the car may be
impounded pending payment of bail (see Motoring).

It is advisable to make photocopies of your travel documents   N.B.
and take them with you. This makes it easier to get replace-
ments if you lose the originals.

181

Walking

With their varied scenery, luxuriant vegetation and excellent climate, the western Canaries offer magnificent walking country.

On Tenerife there are numerous waymarked routes, particularly in the Orotava Valley, the Teide National Park and the Anaga and Teno Hills. The very useful green ICONA maps, issued free of charge by tourist information offices (see Information), show walking routes in the different parts of Tenerife. On the smaller islands the walks are not usually waymarked: in these circumstances a good walkers' guide and a compass are essential requirements.

On Tenerife guided walks are organized by the large travel agencies and by a number of smaller firms. On Gomera, Hierro and La Palma enquire at the local information office.

Some travel firms offer regular walking holidays in the Canaries, covering accommodation and guided walks, sometimes confined to a single island but sometimes also taking in a number of islands.

Long walks should be undertaken only with proper equipment. The paths are sometimes rough and stony, requiring stout footwear, preferably boots. For protection against the strong sun a hat and sun cream are essential. In view of possible changes in the weather some protection against rain should be taken, and in winter warm clothing is necessary.

A very useful and attractive guide to walks on Tenerife is Noel Rochford's "Landscapes of Tenerife" (Sunflower Books, London 1984).

When to go

The Canaries are sometimes called the "islands of eternal spring" – a reputation they owe to a climate which remains equable throughout the year (see Facts and Figures – Climate).

The temperature variation between the coldest month (January) and the warmest (August) is only 6·4 °C (11·5 °F), and bathing is possible all year round. During the winter months, therefore, the islands attract large numbers of visitors from sun-starved Central and Northern Europe. It should, of course, be borne in mind that, particularly in winter, there can be a good deal of cloud and heavy rain on the north coast of Tenerife and the east coasts of Gomera, Hierro and La Palma; the south and west sides of the islands are much sunnier.

From the point of view of vegetation a good time to visit the Canaries is in March, when the flora of the islands is seen in all its splendour.

While in winter accommodation on the Canaries must be booked well in advance, during the summer many hotels are almost empty. However, Tenerife, Gomera, Hierro and La Palma are also very agreeable at this time of year, when oppressively hot and sultry days are rare.

Index

In the tourist resorts on Tenerife visitors are frequently invited to have themselves photographed with an animal – usually an engaging young monkey or lion cub. Before agreeing to any such proposal they should bear in mind that the animals will usually have been sedated with drugs and that they will often have been smuggled into the country in conditions of some cruelty and without any medical check.

Notes

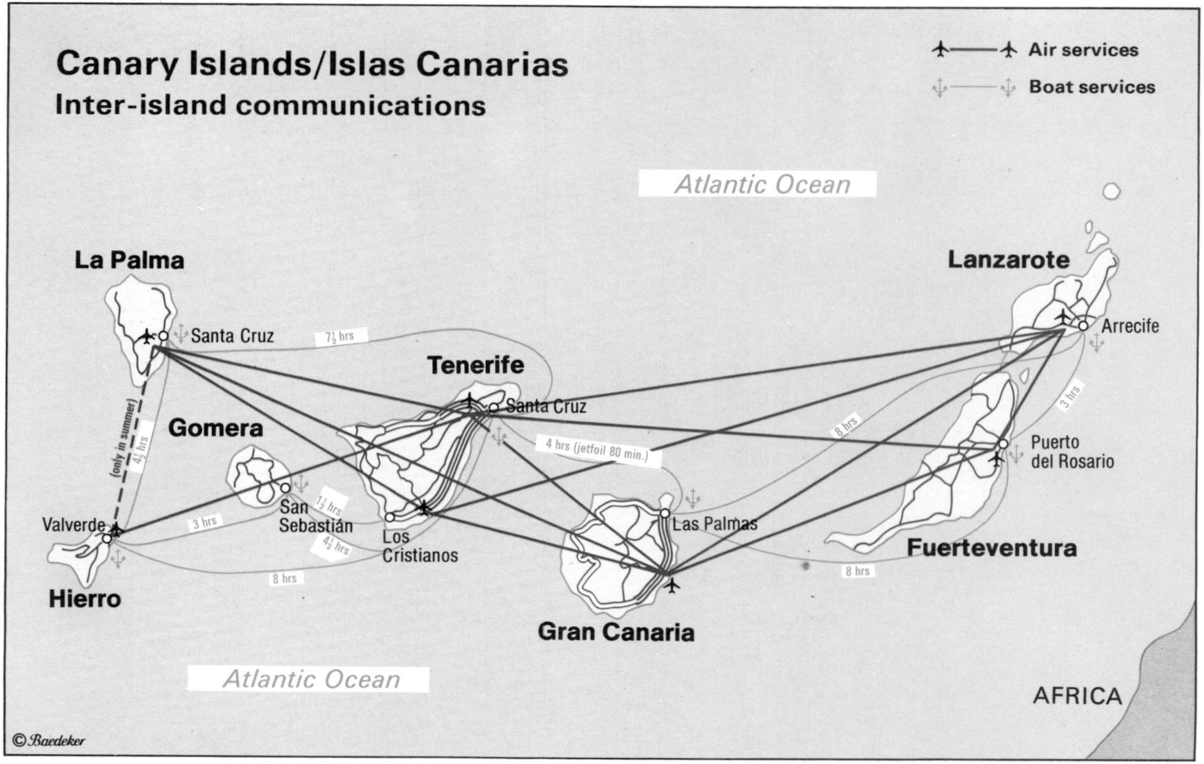

Canary Islands/Islas Canarias
Inter-island communications

Air services

Boat services

Atlantic Ocean

Lanzarote

Arrecife

Puerto del Rosario

3 hrs

Fuerteventura

8 hrs

AFRICA

Las Palmas

Gran Canaria

8 hrs

Santa Cruz

4 hrs (jetfoil 80 min.)

Tenerife

Los Cristianos

La Palma

Santa Cruz

7½ hrs

Gomera

San Sebastián

1½ hrs

4½ hrs

8 hrs

3 hrs

4½ hrs

(only in summer)

Valverde

Hierro

Atlantic Ocean

© Baedeker